PREPPER'S COMMUNICATION HANDBOOK

PREPPER'S COMMUNICATION HANDBOOK

LIFESAVING STRATEGIES FOR STAYING IN CONTACT DURING AND AFTER A DISASTER

JIM COBB

ULYSSES PRESS

Published in the US by:
Ulysses Press
P.O. Box 3440
Berkeley, CA 94703
www.ulyssespress.com

ISBN: 978-1-61243-531-2
Library of Congress Control Number: 2015944214

Printed in the United States

10 9 8 7 6 5 4 3 2 1

Acquisitions editor: Keith Riegert
Managing editor: Claire Chun
Editor: Renee Rutledge
Proofreader: Lauren Harrison
Index: Sayre Van Young
Front cover design: what!design @ whatweb.com
Interior design: Jake Flaherty
Cover artwork: radio communication © Thanakorn Sisongkram/
    shutterstock.com; radio transciever © Aubord Dulac/shutterstock.
    com; antenna © serato/shutterstock.com; ham radio © supersaiyan3/
    shutterstock.com
Interior photos: © copyright Jim Cobb; page 29 © copyright Oliver
    Jenkins/shutterstock.com

For Tammy – Always

CONTENTS

INTRODUCTION

Anyone who has attended one of my classes or sat through one of my convention appearances has heard me say numerous times, "Prepping gives you options." When you get right down to it, that's sort of the whole point. When you take the time to set supplies and gear aside as well as learn and practice relevant skills, you gain the luxury of options when something adverse occurs in your life. Rather than being locked into a single course of action because you lack alternatives, you can adjust your plan and reaction according to the resources available to you.

Information is a critical resource. You need it in order to make effective decisions. Information will, or at least should, guide your actions and your planning. Food, water, and shelter are your first priorities, as those are the things that will keep you alive. But once you have those squared away, you'll need to plan your next move. To do that, you'll need up-to-date and accurate information.

The discussion of emergency communication in this book largely focuses on available options. I'm not going to get into radio theory, physics, propagation, and all that other fun stuff. Instead, I'm going to cover several different types or categories of tools available to you when it comes to communicating both before and after a disaster strikes. I've written this book to be accessible to the widest audience possible. While it may be interesting and worthwhile to learn, you don't need to know how an antenna works to be able to use a radio.

After covering a myriad of communication options, I'll move into communication skills, such as conflict resolution and interpreting body language. A lack of proper communication is at or near the top of the list of reasons we get into arguments with other people. Arguments aren't always based on disagreeing. Often, once you've managed to sit down and have a conversation with someone, you'll find you agree on far more topics than you disagree. The challenge is getting to that point. Knowing how to defuse a conflict, uncover the actual agenda at work behind the scenes, and keep your own information protected are all vital skills I'll cover here.

Take the time to practice and play around with your chosen communication tools. Sure, most of you are familiar with using your smartphones and tablets, but if you're new to the world of amateur, CB, and shortwave radio, you need to get yourself up to speed now, before those skills are put to the test. These aren't tools you can pick up and use intelligently without some serious practice first. Not only do you need to know how and when to use them, you need to learn their limitations. Doing otherwise is sort of like planning to hunt deer with a 9-millimeter pistol. Sure, if you're *really* lucky, you might be able to pull it off. But the odds are against you.

Don't gamble with the lives of your family. Take the time to put each and every communication tool you purchase to the test. Know how to use them in good times as well as under stress. Teach your family members, too, in case you end up away from home when disaster hits.

Have fun with this stuff, folks. It isn't meant to be dry and boring. Think about it like this—practicing with your communication tools can help you find and network with other preppers in your area. Who knows, maybe you'll make a new friend or two!

Chapter 1

ONE-WAY RADIO: RECEIVERS

Most of you already have one or more radios kicking around the house, even if it is just the one in the car or truck. I'll start the journey through prepper communication options with one-way radios, which are thusly named because information only flows one way—to you from the broadcasting channel or station.

AM/FM

AM/FM radio has been omnipresent for decades and is the first thing that comes to mind when the topic of radio comes up. Despite recent advances in technology, there is still something to be said for good, old-fashioned broadcast radio.

BASIC TYPES OF RADIOS

Broadcast radio has been in the United States since around the 1920s. Since then, it has evolved from a hobby enjoyed by those who could puzzle out the complexities of radio equipment to a major force in family entertainment. Nowadays, it seems as though radio often plays second (or perhaps third) fiddle to other means of information transmission. Certainly television supplanted radio's position as the chief entertainer in the household from about the 1950s through the early 2000s. Of course, you can't discount the impact of video streaming and other online mediums, either. There are four basic categories of radios:

- **Handheld.** These are small radios, roughly the size of a walkie-talkie.
- **Mobile.** These radios are installed in vehicles, somewhat akin to CB radios in semis (see page 26).
- **Portable.** These rigs are larger than handheld units but can still be easily carried to different locations.
- **Base.** These radios are large and stationary. They have the most output power but also consume the most resources to operate.

AM stands for amplitude modulation. As the name would imply, an AM signal is one in which the amplitude, or peak of the transmission wave, is modulated or varied. Most of AM broadcasts consist of talk radio, sports, and religious discussions, with a bit of music tossed in here and there across the dial. It has been that way for the last few decades and likely won't be changing any time soon. AM channels range from 540 kHz to 1,700 kHz, spaced at every 10 kHz. For the uninitiated, kHz stands for kilohertz.

For many, AM radio is pretty much a snooze-fest. Not a lot goes on there that gets the blood pumping, other than the occasional ball game.

However, there is an interesting twist to AM radio. For the most part, the broadcasts are local. In the middle of the afternoon, you're going to be tuning in to shows being broadcast within 200 miles or so. But when the sun goes down, the ionosphere changes and, as a result, the AM radio waves can travel much farther, perhaps 500 miles or more. This is easily tested by sitting in your car during the day and scrolling through the AM dial, then repeating the process late at night. You'll likely hear far more broadcasts by the light of the moon.

Westminster Model 1425 Multi-Band Receiver

This multi-band receiver was found for a couple of dollars at a rummage sale. It will tune in not only the standard AM/FM and shortwave transmissions but also weather alert stations, some police frequencies, and CB radio. It is rather old but still works very well.

Why is this notable? If the disaster at hand were regional, local news stations might not have the capacity to broadcast. But stations from outside the affected area will certainly share the information they're able to gather, and it is from them that you might learn more about what's going on.

FM stands for frequency modulation. With AM signals, the frequency remains constant and the amplitude changes, but with FM, the frequency is varied. For most people, this part of the radio dial is most familiar. In the United States, full-power FM stations run from 88.1 to 107.9 MHz. Because of the way the channels are allocated, the frequency will always end in an odd number. Those who routinely listen to broadcast radio hear the bulk of their music and news on these channels.

FM channels are always local affairs. The average range for the higher-powered stations is about 100 to 150 miles. FM stations are great for entertainment and news, provided the news isn't affecting your immediate area.

AM/FM radios are obviously extremely common. Odds are you have several at your disposal already, such as the radio sitting in your kitchen or in the garage workshop.

SATELLITE RADIO

In the last several years, satellite radio has become extremely popular. It is subscription based and, of course, a satellite radio is required to receive the broadcasts. The great thing about satellite radio is the sheer entertainment value. I spend a lot of time in my car and have grown to love the diverse range of options I have with my Sirius subscription. Most of the channels are focused on one specific genre, such as old-time radio shows, 1980s hair metal, or even Jimmy Buffett–style beach music. Naturally, there are all sorts of news stations, too, like CNN.

One of the downsides is the expense. The subscription alone can be costly, unless you're able to negotiate a lower figure. I've never paid full price for my satellite radio subscription.

I just tell my provider that I can't afford whatever they tell me the going rate is, and they'll keep moving the number down until I'm comfortable with it. Granted, were she alive today, my grandmother would give me grief for paying for radio, but at least I'm not shelling out $100 a month for it.

I wouldn't recommend satellite radio as your primary means of collecting information, but if you already subscribe to it, consider adding a small, portable receiver to your bag of tricks. If nothing else, you should be able to download and install a satellite radio app on your phone or tablet. If you go that route, be sure to verify that your subscription plan will allow you to use the radio in your vehicle as well as the portable one.

SHORTWAVE

Shortwave (SW) transmissions can be sent around the world by bouncing them off of the ionosphere, so named because of the high concentration of ions in this strata of the atmosphere, roughly 50 to 600 miles from the Earth's surface. This ion-rich environment allows you to tune in to broadcasts from all over the place. SW, unlike amateur (HAM) radio, is one way. A station transmits and you receive. You aren't able to communicate back on an SW radio.

Most SW broadcasts are prerecorded. They might consist of music, talk, or even just a mysterious voice rattling off numbers (Google "shortwave numbers station"). History has shown that SW broadcasts are generally free of censorship, even in countries where violations of radio silence carry severe punishment. Therefore, a SW broadcast is likely to contain reliable facts, at least as far as the broadcaster believes them to be true.

Of course, there's always the possibility of rumor being reported as fact. You've got to take the good with the bad. The key part of SW for your purposes is that the overseas broadcasts likely won't be designed strictly to keep people calm and thus won't be sanitized or edited to withhold the very information you'll be seeking.

Kaito Voyager Pro Emergency Radio

One of the best emergency radios on the market today is the Kaito Voyager Pro. It is powered by batteries, crank, or the small solar panel you see on top. It will tune in AM/FM/SW and weather radio stations. It can power your cell phone via a small USB port, plus an LED flashlight and SOS emergency light.

Some SW radios allow the user to listen to various HAM frequencies as well. Again, though, the SW radio is a listen-only device. Look for a designation of single sideband (SSB) when researching SW radios. Sideband is what HAM operators use to transmit voice. Occasionally, it will be labeled upper sideband and lower sideband (USB/LSB). With these options, the transmitting signal utilizes a carrier frequency to communicate the audio signal. Two additional signals that are mirror images of one another go along for the ride on either side of the carrier signal. These are the upper and lower sidebands and where the information being relayed actually resides in the transmission. A SSB receiver is able to decode the sideband transmissions into an audible signal. Again, I'm only talking about a SW receiver, not any sort of transmitter, so this is only for gathering information, not sending anything out.

SW radio listening can be a very fun hobby. Many people keep track of the different stations they find—this is called DXing. One resource for finding broadcasts is PrimeTimeShortwave.com. There, you can find broadcasts from all over the world. Another resource is ShortwaveSchedule.com. You might also consider purchasing the *World Radio TV Handbook*, a best-selling directory of global broadcasting. A new edition is issued every year.

Sony ICF-5900W Multi-Band Receiver
This multi-band receiver was inherited from my father and is roughly 40 years old. It still works great for listening to AM/FM and some shortwave transmissions.

NOAA

NOAA stands for National Oceanic and Atmospheric Administration, which many people think of as the weather radio stations. Indeed, one of the primary functions of the NOAA radio stations is to broadcast weather reports. These reports are typically far more detailed and accurate than the ones you'll see on TV.

NOAA weather broadcasts are updated every few hours, more frequently if conditions warrant. They are repeated every 5 minutes, give or take, 24 hours a day, 365 days a year.

The broadcasts you'll hear are for your local area, not some far-flung city.

In order to listen to NOAA broadcasts, you'll need either a specific type of receiver called a "weather radio" or a radio that specifies it will receive weather band broadcasts. Most radios marketed as "emergency radios" will receive the NOAA broadcasts in addition to AM/FM, and sometimes shortwave (SW). Here's where it gets interesting. Many weather radios sold today have what is called Specific Area Message Encoding, or SAME, as well as an alarm of some sort. National Weather Service forecasters

Eton FR-300 Emergency Radio
This radio not only receives AM/FM and shortwave transmissions but weather alerts as well. Crank power means you don't have to rely on batteries. Plus, there's a small flashlight built in to the unit.

can, when necessary, insert a signal that activates the alarm feature of weather alert radios in the affected area. Given the NOAA broadcast system design, if a warning were issued for your area and your radio were turned on, you'd be alerted to the danger with a tonal alarm or other signal.

In 1975, the NOAA system was formally designated as the only government-operated radio system for sending out warnings related to natural disasters, nuclear attack, and other such emergencies. It remains so today. In other words, your weather radio is one of the primary ways you may be warned of an impending disaster. And you thought it was mostly for seeing if the weather is going to be nice enough for a picnic later!

RADIO SCANNER

Sometimes referred to as a police scanner, a radio scanner is awesome for gathering information from a variety of sources, including government agencies and private businesses. It works somewhat like a standard radio in that you need to tune it to specific frequencies in order to listen (see Programming a Radio Scanner on page 16). Once programmed, it will scan those frequencies, pausing any time it detects radio traffic. You could forgo the programming and let it scroll through every single frequency, but that could take a while.

Radio Shack PRO-64 Scanner
This is an older model radio scanner but still quite useful for listening to interagency communications.

There are two types of radios scanners: handheld and desktop. I strongly advise you to go with a handheld model. You're going to want something portable should you need to evacuate. As you research different models, be aware that handheld units don't usually come with an AC power cord. Fortunately, power adapters are readily available. Otherwise, you'll be relying upon battery power, and a radio scanner can eat through quite a few batteries if you keep it powered up constantly.

PHONETIC ALPHABETS

Because there are several letters in the English alphabet that sound very similar to one another, such as B, D, and T, most law enforcement agencies as well as other government departments use a phonetic alphabet when transmitting over the air. There are two primary alphabets, one used by military and aviation and the other by law enforcement.

LETTER	MILITARY/AVIATION	LAW ENFORCEMENT
A	Alpha	Adam
B	Bravo	Boy
C	Charlie	Charles
D	Delta	David
E	Echo	Edward
F	Foxtrot	Frank
G	Golf	George
H	Hotel	Henry
I	India	Ida
J	Juliet	John
K	Kilo	King
L	Lima	Lincoln
M	Mike	Mary
N	November	Nora
O	Oscar	Ocean
P	Papa	Peter
Q	Quebec	Queen
R	Romeo	Robert
S	Sierra	Sam
T	Tango	Tom
U	Uniform	Union
V	Victor	Victor
W	Whiskey	William
X	X-ray	X-ray
Y	Yankee	Young
Z	Zulu	Zebra

10 CODES

The 10 Codes were developed to create a shorthand method of communicating between officers and dispatchers. More and more law enforcement agencies are moving away from the 10 Codes and just using plain talk when communicating via radio. However, it is still a good idea to keep a chart of the codes handy as the move to plain talk certainly isn't universal from coast to coast.

10-0 Caution

10-1 Unable to copy transmission

10-2 Signal good/strong

10-3 Stop transmitting

10-4 Acknowledgment (OK)

10-5 Relay

10-6 Busy

10-7 Out of service

10-8 In service

10-9 Repeat

10-10 Fight in progress

10-11 Dog case

10-12 Stand by (stop)

10-13 Weather or traffic report

10-14 Prowler report

10-15 Civil disturbance

10-16 Domestic disturbance

10-17 Meet complainant

10-18 Quickly

10-19 Return to [location]

10-20 Location

10-21 Call [person] by telephone

10-22 Disregard

10-23 Arrived at scene

10-24 Assignment completed

10-25 Meet with [person]

10-26 Detaining subject

10-27 Driver's license information

10-28 Vehicle registration information

10-29 Check for warrants

10-30 Unnecessary use of radio

10-31 Crime in progress

10-32 Man with gun

10-33 Emergency

10-34 Riot

10-35 Major crime alert

10-36 Correct time

10-37 Suspicious vehicle

10-38 Stopping suspicious vehicle

10-39 Urgent: use light, siren

10-40 Silent run: no light, siren

10-41 Beginning tour of duty

10-42 Ending tour of duty

10-43 Information

10-44 Permission to leave

10-45 Animal carcass

10-46 Assist motorist

10-47 Emergency road repairs

10-48 Traffic standard repair

10-49 Traffic light out at ...

10-50 Traffic accident

10-51 Wrecker needed

10-52 Ambulance needed

10-53 Road blocked

10-54 Livestock on highway

10-55 Suspected DUI

10-56 Intoxicated pedestrian

10-57 Hit and run

10-58 Direct traffic

10-59 Convoy or escort

10-60 Squad in vicinity

10-61 Personnel in vicinity

10-62 Reply to message

10-63 Prepare to make written copy

10-64 Message for local delivery

10-65 Net message assignment

10-66 Message cancellation

10-67 Clear for net message

10-68 Dispatch information

10-69 Message received

10-70 Fire

10-71 Advise nature of fire

10-72 Report progress on fire

10-73 Smoke report

10-74 Negative

10-75 In contact with [person]

10-76 En route to [location]

10-77 Estimated time of arrival (ETA)

10-78 Need assistance

10-79 Notify coroner

10-80 Chase in progress

10-81 Breathalyzer

10-82 Reserve lodging

10-83 Work school crossing

10-84 If meeting, advise ETA

10-85 Delayed due to [reason]

10-86 Officer/operator on duty

10-87 Pick up/distribute checks

10-88 Present telephone number

10-89 Bomb threat

10-90 Bank alarm

10-91 Pick up prisoner/ subject

10-92 Improperly parked vehicle

10-93 Blockade

10-94 Drag racing

10-95 Prisoner/subject in custody

10-96 Mental subject

10-97 Check (test) signal

10-98 Prison/jail break

10-99 Wanted/stolen indicated

More and more government agencies, such as police and fire departments, are moving from analog, such as AM or FM signals, to digital systems for their interagency communications. This means you'll need to invest in a digital radio scanner to hear what's going on. Digital scanners are far more expensive than the analog ones, so be forewarned. However, even if all you can afford is an analog scanner, all is not lost. See, the hidden value of a radio scanner is that with a little bit of homework, you can listen in on far more than just emergency services.

One of the most popular resources for radio communications data is RadioReference.com. There, you can find common to relatively obscure frequencies in use in your local area. For example, I checked for those in my home county and found not only fire, police, and rescue departments but frequencies used by my town's Department of Public Works (DPW), the security staff at a local resort, and even a school bus company. Those could be useful because the DPW and bus drivers are on the roads every day and their radio conversations could clue me in on weather conditions and traffic. The resort security radio traffic? Well, you just never know where the zombie uprising might start. Private businesses are far less likely to be cautious about the information they discuss on the radio, too, so you might glean a bit of information that would otherwise be kept off the air.

Programming a Radio Scanner

Nowadays, many scanners can be programmed quite easily using readily available software. In the days before home computers became commonplace, frequencies had to be keyed into the unit by hand. While you could save them as channels and organize them into user-defined sections called banks, it was still rather tedious. That said, I recommend you make a list of all the frequencies you program into your scanner. Hand keying is still an option and may be necessary should the scanner somehow lose memory and you don't have access to a computer for reprogramming.

Most radio scanners today allow you to save at least a few hundred channels or frequencies. Designate one or two banks for local frequencies. Bear in mind that some agencies will have multiple frequencies. For example, a police department might have one frequency for dispatch, another for car-to-car communication, and another for handheld scanners.

Use a resource like RadioReference.com to find the frequencies listed for agencies in your local area. At a minimum, program the frequencies for local police, fire, and rescue departments. I suggest you also include the county sheriff's department and any local hospital security departments. At the state level, include:

- Department of Transportation
- Department of Natural Resources
- Department of Health
- State Police

There are also several federal-level agencies from which you might glean valuable information. These include:

- Federal Bureau of Investigation (FBI)
- Drug Enforcement Agency (DEA)
- Bureau of Alcohol, Tobacco, Firearms, and Explosives (ATF)
- National Park Service
- US Marshals
- Department of Homeland Security (DHS)
- Federal Emergency Management Agency (FEMA)

Many law enforcement agencies utilize encryption or coding when discussing sensitive information via radio. In my area, what you'll hear is an officer or dispatcher saying, "Go to coded." The transmission that follows will then be static or garbled until they switch back. They do this most often when the information being transmitted involves a juvenile's name or the complaint being addressed is of a rather sensitive nature. I point this out because if you didn't know this ahead of time, you might fear your scanner is on the fritz when a transmission suddenly goes static.

Even after programming all of those frequencies, you'll likely still have plenty of space available. Break out your bug out plan (you *do* have a bug out plan, right?). Use your maps to make a list of all of the towns, big and small, that you'll travel near or through when bugging out. Seek out and program the applicable radio frequencies for the police and other emergency services for each of those towns. This way, should you end up having to bug out, you can stay abreast of developments during your travels, including valuable information concerning possible roadblocks or other obstacles.

Chapter 2

TWO-WAY RADIO

During any situation, gathering information is extremely important and is the first step in communication. You will likely want to be able to send and receive, being active rather than passive. That's where two-way communication comes into play. Telephones are the obvious first choice when it comes to two-way communication. But, as we'll see, they certainly aren't the only option. Handheld radios come in a few different types, each with its advantages and disadvantages.

Before I get too far into the different options available, it's important for me to address the issue of power.

POWER

No matter what kind of radio(s) you end up purchasing, you will need a way to keep them powered up if the wall outlets fail to work as a result of the disaster. For handhelds, batteries will be your best, and possibly only, option. Choose a radio that will accept standard AA or AAA batteries, though quite often, the batteries will have to be placed into a special pack. An excellent investment is a small solar panel, such as those sold by SunJack or Goal Zero, along with a battery charger. These work very well at ensuring you always have a fresh set of batteries on hand.

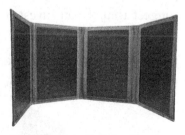

SunJack 14-watt Solar Charger
I've been using it for almost two years now, and it works great for charging tablets, cell phones, and batteries.

Something else to consider when looking at chargers for your handheld's battery packs: The chargers come in two types. Either the charger cable will run from the radio to the wall outlet, or it will run from the outlet to a special "drop in" charger, where you take the battery pack from the radio and place it into the charger. The latter type will charge the battery far faster than the other, something you may want to consider.

Goal Zero Battery Charger
Hook up a battery charger to your solar panel and you're good to go.

On top of that, see if there is an automotive charger available for your radio, the kind of charger that plugs into the cigarette lighter in your car. Whether you end up mobile or not, using this charger will help conserve your batteries.

For the larger rigs, many can be run using DC power, such as from a car battery, with special cables. I would highly suggest that if you invest in a base unit, you find out how to run it in this way, just in case. It makes little sense to buy radio equipment to use in an emergency, then have no way to use it when the emergency actually happens.

WakaWaka Emergency Light
The oddly named flashlight and power charger in one is an excellent option for keeping your phone or tablet powered up. One side (left) is a small solar panel, while the other side (right) has two very bright LED lights. The single button, shown in the center, cycles the lights through different levels of illumination. The USB port on the side allows you to charge a cell phone, tablet, or other device.

TELEPHONES

Every one of you out there reading this book is no doubt familiar with telephones. Even if you're one of the very few human beings who doesn't have a cell phone in their pocket, I'm quite sure you've seen them before. When push comes to shove, I'd bet you can figure out how to operate one. Therefore, I'm not going to devote much space at all to the telephone as a communication tool. There are, however, a couple of things to consider.

Cell towers can quickly become overwhelmed in an emergency. While you might very well have a strong signal reaching your phone, calls won't go through because of the sheer number of calls being placed. We've seen this happen time after time during major emergencies. However, quite often, text messages will still get through. This is due to how the networks are designed. If you can't get a call through to your family, shoot them a text and see if that works.

Failing that, if you have a smartphone and can get an Internet connection, try some of the suggestions outlined in Chapter 4, Online Communication.

Many people have begun exploring satellite phones, too. Satellite phones, or satphones, are another option for the prepper concerned about being able to communicate during or after a disaster. Today's satphones are often almost

SOLAR LANDSCAPE LIGHTS

Solar landscape lights are everywhere, lining front walks and backyard paths of many a home. Not only do these lights create a little ambience for the patio area, they can be used to recharge batteries. Many use AA batteries. The small solar panel charges the battery throughout the day, then the battery powers the light all night. You can replace the generic battery inside with one of your own rechargeable ones. When the sun sets, take the battery out and use it where needed.

By the way, in a pinch you could use solar landscape lights to provide illumination inside the home during a power outage. They won't provide a ton of light, of course, but it'll be enough to keep you from tripping over the coffee table.

indistinguishable from a common cell phone in appearance, though they don't often have a full touch screen. Satphones tend to be a bit more expensive than a normal cell phone, too, with prices ranging from $200 to $2,000 or more.

Unlike cell phones, which use towers to communicate, as the name would imply, a satellite phone uses satellites. Satphones are also built to utilize a specific network and

RULES FOR SUCCESSFUL TWO-WAY RADIO COMMUNICATION

Over the decades, a few established rules have been developed, and they go a long way toward providing successful radio communication between two or more parties. These rules aren't part of any official code and you won't find them on a written test. Someone, however, will likely chastise you should you violate one of them.

Take turns speaking. If two people talk at once, neither will hear the other. You need to wait a moment to be sure the other person has finished speaking before keying your own microphone. To do otherwise is to risk "stepping" on the other person. A great way to ensure this doesn't happen to you is to get into the habit of saying "Over" when your message is complete.

Keep transmissions short and to the point. Know what you're going to say before you start transmitting. Avoid long, rambling monologues about this, that, and the other thing. First, it is really annoying to listeners. Second, other parties might have information they are trying to communicate but can't because you're going on and on about just how awesome the sunset was three weeks ago.

Make sure your microphone's transmit key is off when you finish speaking. Countless times, I've heard someone cannot be switched to another one. At this time, there are only a handful of companies providing satellite communication service, with some of them only servicing specific parts of the globe.

The good news is that a satphone won't be affected by a cell network clogged with panicked calls and texts during a crisis. The bad news is that you're going to pay through

transmit a question and then is unable to hear any replies because their transmit button got stuck. For clarification, the transmit key is the button you push and hold down while speaking. When you are done speaking, you need to release the transmit key so your radio can receive incoming transmissions. The transmit key is usually located along the side of the radio, often where your fingers or thumb would naturally fall while holding the radio. Failing to release the transmit key could also result in background conversations on your end being transmitted over the air, which could be slightly embarrassing, or perhaps far worse, depending on what was said and who was listening.

Double-check the channel or frequency before transmitting on it for the first time each day. Make this habit a part of your routine. It can be far too easy to misread a number and end up sending out potentially sensitive information on the wrong channel.

Act like a station. Last but not least, according to accepted radio jargon, if you are using radio transmission gear, you are considered a "station." Whether you have $10,000 in equipment and a 40-foot antenna or it is just you, a handheld CB radio, and a bag of Cheetos, you're a station, so straighten up and act like it.

the nose for that luxury. Expect to pay as much as $2 per minute, perhaps even more, depending upon the plan you choose. Data is also costly.

Another consideration is the fact that more and more members of the media are investing in satellite phones and usage plans so that they can communicate with their home offices and such while they are in the field covering disasters. This means the once relatively unpopulated satellite services are getting a bit more crowded as time goes on.

Call quality is subjective to the strength of the signal you receive from the satellite. The length of your calls may also be hampered because you and the satellite are both constantly moving and the signal could be easily dropped.

That said, a satphone might be your best option if you're heading out into the wilderness, far from any cell towers. If nothing else, a satphone can be a lifesaving backup should your plans go awry. They are an expensive option but your circumstances just might warrant the investment.

CITIZEN'S BAND RADIO

Those of you who were around in the 1970s will no doubt remember the Citizen's Band (CB) radio craze that swept the country. It seemed like everyone and their brother had a mic hanging from the dashboard, whether they were driving a big rig, pickup truck, or wood-paneled station wagon. It had to make many truckers chuckle to hear housewives

CB POPULARITY IN THE 1970S

We have oil to thank for the crazy popularity of CB radios in the 1970s, believe it or not. Here's the quick-and-dirty history lesson behind it. In 1973, in retaliation for the support that the United States and some Western European countries were giving Israel, the Organization of the Petroleum Exporting Countries, better known as OPEC, declared an oil embargo. Gas prices soared and the US government eventually instituted a national highway speed limit of 55 miles per hour as a means of conserving fuel usage.

Truck drivers were unhappy about the speed limit change because it affected how many loads they could handle in a given timeframe. The rising cost of fuel also had a huge impact. So, they took to the CB airwaves to help one another find cheap gas and avoid speed traps. They also occasionally used their radios to organize protests, such as blockades and slow-moving convoys. Naturally, this spilled over into popular culture with movies like *Smokey and the Bandit* as well as *Convoy*. As people saw CBs used in the movies, many decided they wanted to share in the fun themselves.

calling out things like, "Breaker one-nine, this is Pink Flamingo. Anyone out there got their ears on?"

CB radios utilize a total of 40 channels. Each channel is considered open, meaning anyone can transmit on them. However, channel 9 is understood to be for emergency use only. Channel 19 is typically the most popular channel and where you're likely to hear the most traffic.

CB is used for both personal and business purposes, though it is far more popular among truck drivers than any other segment of the population. They use CBs to keep in contact with one another, checking for weather and road conditions as well as for the presence of radar-running law enforcement.

The learning curve for using a CB radio is pretty short. One simply sets the radio to a channel, picks up the mic, presses the transmit key, and talks. The downside is that CB radios generally have a very limited range. Several factors affect the transmitting and receiving range, including the height of the antenna, the surrounding terrain, and the radio's power. On flat ground, a good-quality base radio with a properly installed antenna might get you as much as 50 miles. For the average person with a vehicle installed unit traveling through some hills rather than standing in the middle of Flat-as-a-Pane-of-Glass, Nebraska, you're looking at a range of about 5 miles or so.

Cobra HH34 Handheld CB Radio

A handheld CB radio won't have nearly as much range as a vehicle-installed model, owing to the smaller antenna on the handheld. But if you're near a major highway, you can still pick up some transmissions.

FRS/GMRS

Walkie-talkies have come a long way since I played army as a kid. In the mid-1990s, the Federal Communications Commission (FCC) authorized the use of 14 frequencies initially intended for families, giving them the name Family Radio Service (FRS), but as time went on, more and more businesses jumped on the bandwagon, too. The idea was to set aside a group of frequencies with no license application, test, or other red tape required for use. Basically, to enable a consumer to buy a set of two-way radios and use them to communicate with family members, such as when attending special events.

Prior to the FRS coming into being, there was the General Mobile Radio Service (GMRS), which arose from the Citizens Radio Service. Not to be mistaken with Citizens Band radio, the Citizens Radio Service came about in the 1960s for both individuals and businesses to use. As time went on, the frequencies became cluttered as more and more users signed on. Finally, in the 1970s, a set of channels or frequencies were removed from the Citizens Radio  Service and designated Business Radio Service. The Citizen Radio Service name was then changed to the current GMRS.

The GMRS differs from the FRS in a couple of ways. First, you need to be licensed in order to legally transmit on GMRS frequencies. There is no exam for this license, just a form and a fee. Second, GMRS radios are allowed to use more power than their FRS counterparts, thus giving them a bit more range.

All told, there are 22 frequencies allotted for FRS and GMRS radios. The first seven are shared between the two, the next seven are for FRS use only, and the rest are for GMRS use only.

So, to recap, there are two primary flavors of handheld two-way radios today, FRS and GMRS. FRS use requires no license and the radios are comparatively inexpensive. GMRS requires a license but the radios are more powerful than FRS, allowing for greater range.

To confuse things, some manufacturers produce radios capable of receiving and transmitting on both FRS and GMRS frequencies. While these relatively inexpensive two-way radios have their uses in the overall communication plan, you have to consider their limitations. For starters, despite manufacturer claims, you're not likely to see an effective range of 10 miles, let alone the 20 or even 30 miles you'll see listed on the package. In fact, in most parts of the country, if you can get a mile-long range with an FRS radio and a

CHANNELS

Shared		FRS Only		GMRS Only	
1	462.5625 MHz	8	467.5625 MHz	15	462.5500 MHz
2	462.5875 MHz	9	467.5875 MHz	16	462.5750 MHz
3	462.6125 MHz	10	467.6125 MHz	17	462.6000 MHz
4	462.6375 MHz	11	467.6375 MHz	18	462.6250 MHz
5	462.6625 MHz	12	467.6625 MHz	19	462.6500 MHz
6	462.6875 MHz	13	467.6875 MHz	20	462.6750 MHz
7	462.7125 MHz	14	467.7125 MHz	21	462.7000 MHz
				22	462.7250 MHz

2-mile range with a GMRS one, you're doing pretty well. These radios operate on line of sight, which means anything that interrupts your sight line, including trees, buildings, and hills, will also interfere with the transmission signal.

MURS

Multi-Use Radio Service (MURS) frequencies are less commonly used than FRS or GMRS frequencies, but I think this has more to do with a lack of awareness than anything else. In 2000, the FCC allocated five frequencies previously used strictly by businesses to be license-free and for public use.

MURS radios are generally handheld models, though larger, stationary base unit models are available. The range with the handhelds is typically around 2 miles, depending on terrain. The base units connect to larger external antennas, allowing for ranges of around 10 miles.

The five frequencies used by MURS are:

151.820 MHz

151.880 MHz

151.940 MHz

154.570 MHz

154.600 MHz

In the grand scheme of things, handheld MURS radios are more powerful than their FRS cousins, giving you longer range. However, GMRS radios will typically reach farther than MURS, at least as when comparing handheld models.

The trade-off is that GMRS frequencies require a license for transmission.

No matter which, if any, of these handheld models (FRS, GMRS, MURS) you choose, a major consideration is the lack of privacy. Anyone with one of these radios, or even a radio scanner, can tune in to any frequency and listen to conversations, provided they are in range. This, however, can work to your advantage. By investing in a set of radios or a scanner, you can monitor the frequencies for those who might be in your neck of the woods. In fact, this is something I highly recommend you do in the event of a serious, long-term situation. We'll talk a bit more about this in a later chapter.

TWO-WAY RADIO ACCESSORIES

As you shop for a two-way radio that will meet your needs, take available accessories and options into consideration. For example, some sort of headset or earpiece would be advisable when using a handheld radio out in the field. I recommend a set of small earbuds. Only use one of them, though, leaving your other ear open and able to easily hear the world around you. Whichever type of earpiece you choose, the idea is that only you will hear what is being received on your radio. Sure, you could turn the volume on the radio way down, but then you will end up having to hold the radio itself to your ear in order to hear what's going on.

Some earpiece accessories incorporate a small microphone along the wire. This is a great option. It allows you to leave the radio clipped to your belt or pack, rather than having to grab it every time you want to transmit.

As mentioned, batteries will be necessary for almost all types of two-way radios. Invest in at least two full sets of batteries for each radio. This gives you one complete set to swap out at any given time, plus a backup set.

If the radio has a removable antenna, consider investing in a second antenna, preferably one larger than the stock version that came with the radio. Longer antennas generally provide longer range as well as better overall reception. Plus, a radio is all but worthless if the antenna is damaged, so you'll want to have a backup.

Chapter 3

AMATEUR RADIO

There are several theories on how amateur radio came to be known as ham radio. One of the most common states that it was originally a derogatory term used by telegraph operators when referring to someone with poor radio skills, suggesting they were "ham-fisted" with the gear. No matter the actual origin, ham radio today has become synonymous with emergency communication.

For many people, the thought of entering the world of ham radio is rather intimidating. There are licenses to acquire, tests to take, and just what is propagation anyway? The good news is that while there is some technical know-how involved, the skills and knowledge necessary to use ham rigs are effectively accessible to just about anyone. If you can tune in to an FM station on your car radio and use a microphone, you can handle working a ham radio—once you've done some studying.

Now, I'm going to warn you right up front. There is far more to know about ham radio than I'm including in this chapter. Honestly, I'm barely going to scratch the surface. The idea in this chapter is to give you a brief overview of what's involved with entering the world of amateur radio. If this is an area you wish to explore further, I highly advise you to network with ham operators in your area as well as avail yourself of the truly massive and informative website for the Amateur Radio Relay League, ARRL.org.

LICENSING

The one major difference between ham radio and most of the other options we've discussed in this book is that broadcasting via amateur radio requires a license. This is nonnegotiable. If you are proven to be broadcasting without the proper license, you face pretty steep fines and possibly jail time. Plus, your gear could be confiscated.

Just about every ham operator out there will report an unlicensed broadcast. The FCC is very good at tracking down unlicensed operators. Truly, it isn't a matter of *if* you'll get caught but *how quickly* it will happen.

There is a school of thought that believes no one is going to care whether you're licensed or not during a major crisis because they'll be too busy with other, more important things. You're probably right. However, using your rig properly requires practice. Ham radio isn't something you can just read about and then do proficiently, and practicing with broadcasting requires a license.

Now, before anyone starts complaining about overregulation and red tape, keep in mind that the United States is far from alone in requiring their amateur radio operators to be licensed. Most countries have some sort of regulation process, some more rigorous than others.

I'll tell you something else, too. I have yet to meet a ham operator who won't bend over backward to help someone new learn the ropes. But, if you're known to be broadcasting without a license, you are persona non grata as far as the legit operators are concerned. Not if, but when, you run into trouble, they're likely not going to come running to your aid.

All licenses are good for 10 years, at which point they must be renewed.

Among other things, the type of license you possess determines the frequencies you're allowed to use. Here in the United States, there are three levels or classes of licensure.

TECHNICIAN This is the basic level and where most ham radio operators get started. It requires the satisfactory completion of a 35-question exam that covers applicable regulations, radio theory, and other such topics. Successful Technician Class licensure allows the operator to communicate locally and, with the right equipment, regionally.

GENERAL This is the next step up from Technician Class. This class of licensure requires the successful completion of the Technician Class level exam as a prerequisite, followed by an additional 35-question exam. The General Class license grants the operator the use of all available frequencies, with the exception of some of the high-frequency (HF) ones. If you plan to communicate globally, this is where you want to be.

EXTRA Using an oxymoron, this is professional amateur level of licensure. If you're serious about the hobby and want to legally do everything and anything related to amateur radio, including the HF frequencies that are off limits to the General class, the Extra Class operator license should be your goal. Getting there won't be easy, though. You'll need to pass both the Technician and General license exams, as well as a 50-question exam. This is heavy-duty material and not for the faint of heart.

Note that none of the license classes require the knowledge or use of Morse code. This was a long-standing requirement that was eliminated. For many, learning Morse code was a stumbling block when it came to studying for the exam. That said, I still encourage the study and occasional practice of Morse code, simply because you never know when it might come in handy.

You'll sometimes hear these exams referred to as "elements." The Technician Class test is called Element 2, General Class is Element 3, and Extra Class is Element 4. Why no

Element 1? Because that was the now-discontinued Morse code test.

Studying for the Test

Here's the good news. You can freely obtain all of the exam questions, and the correct answers, for each level of licensure. They aren't treated like trade secrets, not by a long shot. Each exam draws from a pool of questions that you can access through numerous study guides that will walk you through each and every one.

The pool of questions changes every four years, so you need to make sure the study guide(s) you use are current. Oh, and the questions are all multiple choice, so you know the correct answers will be right in front of you.

Even with the DIY study guides out there, you might consider taking an actual class. Some people learn better with the guidance of a knowledgeable instructor. Plus, it is a good way to meet others who might share your interests. Many ham clubs offer classes throughout the year. Even if they don't have a class scheduled in the immediate future, they'll likely know of other options in your area.

Taking the Test

As of this writing, the test fee is $15. This gives you one attempt at the exam. Fail and you'll have to pay an additional fee to retake the exam. Testing is done at various locations throughout the country. Once upon a time, all testing was done at FCC facilities. Today, not so much. The easiest way to find a testing location and schedule for your area is to search the FCC website (FCC.gov) for the amateur radio license test.

You'll need a score of 75 percent or better to pass the test. You should get your results right after taking the exam

CALL SIGNS

Every licensed ham operator has a call sign that they've either been assigned or have chosen for themselves (called a vanity call sign). Call signs consist of two parts: a prefix that identifies, at minimum, the country assigning the call sign, and a suffix that is the unique identifier for each operator.

For all intents and purposes, you are your call sign. That's your name when broadcasting. As you progress through the different license classes, you will retain the same call sign unless you choose otherwise.

HAM RADIO CLUBS

One of the best ways to learn how to use your gear more effectively as well as network with like-minded people is to join one or more ham radio organizations.

PRO TIP: Many ham operators are also preppers.

Ham clubs can be found from coast to coast. No matter where you live, I'm willing to bet there's a ham club somewhere nearby. Granted, "nearby" can be a relative term. Still,

I doubt there's a county in the country that doesn't have some sort of ham presence.

The easiest way to find a local ham club is to do an Internet search for your county name and "ham radio." If that doesn't net you a good result, expand the search to the counties adjacent to you. Unless you live in an extremely remote area, you'll probably find a club based within an easy drive of your home. You might even find a couple. If possible, check out all of the local clubs to find one that seems to be the best fit for you and your interests. Each club is going to vary a little in size and focus. You might want a small club that concentrates on public service, or a large club that does a lot of contests. It's totally up to you.

NATIONAL INCIDENT MANAGEMENT SYSTEM (NIMS)

As you might imagine, when a disaster is of sufficient magnitude that numerous agencies from all levels of government become involved, there is a great likelihood for confusion and chaos—sort of an example of too many cooks in the kitchen. In 2004, the Department of Homeland Security tackled this very problem and created the National Incident Management System (NIMS). The idea was to provide a framework that takes into account all of the different agencies that could respond to a given disaster, outlining each group's functions and responsibilities.

If you decide to get formally involved with any sort of organized emergency communication group, you will no doubt become well-versed in the NIMS protocols as they apply to your organization. Should you wish to learn more about it on your own, hit up the FEMA website (Fema.gov).

The important thing here is to network with area ham operators. Get to know them and let them get to know you. On the whole, they are great assets and, in my experience, great people.

EMERGENCY COMMUNICATION

Ham operators play a key role in emergency communications during a disaster and its aftermath. One of the largest responses to date was during Hurricane Katrina, when over one thousand ham operators headed to the Gulf Coast. They worked with groups like the Red Cross to facilitate rescue efforts in any way they could. Some operators even functioned as 911 dispatchers in areas where traditional forms of communication had completely failed.

There are two main organizations that ham operators can join to assist with such emergency communication efforts: ARES and RACES.

Amateur Radio Emergency Service (ARES) is the nation's largest ham radio emergency communication organization. It is sponsored by the Amateur Radio Relay League (ARRL). ARES works with both government departments and rescue and aid organizations like the American Red Cross. The group is run by volunteers, and all members receive training in emergency communications.

The **Radio Amateur Civil Emergency Service (RACES)** is what you might think of as the official or governmental equivalent to ARES. RACES is a function of FEMA, though members are volunteers rather than employees. RACES is activated typically only after a disaster has happened and is in use during a very limited duration.

Here are the main differences between ARES and RACES, in a nutshell:

- ARES is run by the ARRL, a civilian entity, whereas RACES is a function of the government, though it is still staffed by volunteers rather than government employees.

- ARES will be in use before, during, and after the disaster. RACES is activated only after the disaster's impact has reached a point where it is directly affecting communication between government agencies.

CONFIGURING YOUR HAM RADIO UNIT

Just as with buying a firearm, knife, or other piece of gear, the type of radio you choose will largely depend upon budget and what you want to do with the item. For example, you wouldn't buy a .22 rifle for big-game hunting in Africa, right? Nor would you want to baton firewood with a Swiss Army knife.

Truth be told, budget takes a backseat to function. Ham radio technology has been around long enough that you should be able to find one in your price range that will handle just about anything you'll want to accomplish.

REPEATERS

Using a ham radio to speak directly to another person is called *simplex* operation. Think of it sort of like communication with walkie-talkies. The signal goes from your radio directly to the other one. Now, here's where ham radio gets cool. You can use repeaters to engage in *duplex* operation. Basically, this consists of sending a signal from your radio to a large antenna in your area, which then rebroadcasts your signal much farther and with greater power than you could broadcast on your own. These repeater antennas are typically installed and maintained by ham clubs or those who are involved with emergency communications in your area.

Repeater towers are usually equipped with generators or some other method of emergency power, too.

Because your primary concern will most likely be with communicating with others during an emergency, rather than setting up a dedicated radio shack (not the store, obviously, but a room devoted to your radio gear) in your basement, a handheld radio might be the best option, at least for a first radio. A handheld radio that uses very high frequency/ultrahigh frequency (VHF/UHF) and has 5 watts of output power will suffice for most needs. Should you end up bitten by the ham bug and you want to expand your rig, feel free.

The antenna is an extremely important component of your ham radio unit. It is a primary determinate of how far you will be able to transmit and the signals you will be able to receive. Most handhelds come equipped with small, fixed antennas. These will do the job, but you'll be better served by investing in an aftermarket whip antenna. This antenna will be placed on your vehicle or some other location, with a cable running from it to your handheld radio. Many of these whip antennas are still small enough that you can easily pack them for transport.

Finally, all radios require some sort of power (see page 20), so be sure you have the supplies needed to keep them running.

DISTRESS CALLS

While hopping on the radio and screaming for help might work, there is an accepted protocol for making a distress call using a ham radio:

> *"Mayday, mayday, mayday, this is [your name and/or call sign]. I am at [location, either address, latitude/longitude, or some other indication of where on Earth you are]."*

You then state the problem, such as a member of your family has had a heart attack, someone is trapped in a collapsed house, or whatever the crisis may be. Continue transmitting this message several times. If you don't receive an answer after several minutes, try transmitting on a different frequency. Obviously, choose frequencies that are most likely to be monitored.

If you hear a distress call, don't ignore it! Do whatever you can to assist. You could be the only human being on the planet who hears the call. The first thing you should do is respond to the call and jot down the date, time, and frequency on which the distress call is transmitted. Get as much information from the caller as possible, including their location and the details of their emergency.

Once you have a location, even if it is somewhat vague, call 911 and advise the dispatcher of what you know. Even if the emergency is happening miles away from you, the dispatcher will likely be in a better position to contact the appropriate agencies.

There is a lot to learn if you're interested in adding amateur radio to your bag of tricks. However, it is certainly worth the effort as you'll be hard-pressed to find another community more devoted to emergency communication. Ham operators, by and large, are not only friendly, but extremely helpful to those who are new to the field.

THE RADIO SHACK

Many people, once they've gotten their feet wet with ham radio, decide to invest in an ever-increasing amount of gear and eventually devote a room, or at least some sort of permanent space, to their ham rig and related equipment. The term "radio shack" stems from the early days of radio, when hobbyists would build their own gear in a garage or other outbuilding. The equipment was often loud, so keeping it out of the house was desired by all involved. The term was also used in the US Navy. The radio equipment was stored and used in small wooden structures that were built either on the deck or above the bridge of a ship.

Today, the term "radio shack" refers to the permanent home for your communications gear, specifically your ham radio rig. It could be in the basement, attic, or somewhere in between. Perhaps the garage or a tool shed will be ideal for you. Even if you don't go so far as to invest in a ton of ham radio gear, having a dedicated spot for your communications equipment will certainly make it easier to find and use it when necessary.

For the purposes of this discussion, the assumption is you've decided to set up a room in your home specifically for communications equipment. What are the ideal parameters or qualities you'll want in such a space?

Start with installing plenty of power outlets. Seriously, you'll want far more than what is currently there. If you're not experienced with this sort of job, I recommend you hire someone who is, preferably a licensed electrician. Communications gear runs on electricity and every piece of equipment you add to the mix is going to need an outlet. One approach to this problem is to install long power strips along the wall at desktop height. This is a great idea as it prevents you from having to bend down and dig behind your desk to get at the various plugs and such.

All of those pieces of equipment will obviously have lots of wires and cords running hither and yon, so plan ahead. Any desks will need to be at least a few inches away from the walls to accommodate all those wires. Invest in Velcro ties or some other means of keeping the cords bunched together and under control. You might also pick up some inexpensive mailing labels. Label each cord on both ends so you know what piece of equipment uses it. This makes things a whole lot easier if you need to unplug a specific cord from a power strip.

You'll need a large work surface, such as a desk or table. Hunt around thrift stores and rummage sales and you should be able to find something that will suit your needs without breaking the bank. Failing that, consider a good-quality folding table from an office supply store. The ones produced today tend to be fairly strong, so they'll support quite a bit of gear. Plus, they come in a variety of sizes so you're sure to find one that will fit your available space. Keep in mind that you need not only a place for your equipment, but for yourself as well. At a minimum, your work surface will need to accommodate the radio, a notebook, a desk lamp, and a cup of coffee. Many operators today include a computer, keyboard, and monitor in the mix, too.

While you're shopping for furniture, buy the most comfortable chair you can afford. I'm serious about this. You'll likely be spending hours and hours monitoring radio traffic and other broadcasts. Doing so while sitting on a cheap folding chair will just make you miserable. I would caution you, though, to make sure the chair you like will fit in the space you have available. If you have thick carpet in your radio shack, a rolling chair isn't going to work very well and you'll end up very frustrated. Either remove the carpet or buy a chair mat.

Shelving is great for organizing your equipment as well as keeping it off of your work surface. Just be sure the shelving will support the weight of the gear. Take care to attach the shelving to wall studs rather than just drywall. Remember, too, that just like with your desk, you're going to need to have wires and cables running here and there. Make sure your shelf system can be set up such that you can leave space between the shelves and the wall for those wires.

In addition to wall shelving, do some web surfing for "kitchen storage" and "kitchen organization" products. You'll find all sorts of shelf risers, tiered shelving, and other items that might work great to keep your gear stowed and yet accessible, leaving you with a larger work area to boot. If you're the handy type, you can probably eyeball products that will meet your needs and then build them yourself.

You'll need to find a way to run one or more antenna cables into your shack. If you're out in a tool shed or other outbuilding, this probably won't be a big issue. If you're in the basement, though, that's a different story. Fortunately, there are a variety of solutions, no matter what your situation might be. Unfortunately, I cannot possibly list them all here. Do some Google searching and you'll find what you seek. Failing that, seek the guidance of experienced ham operators in your area. If you're still stuck for a solution, call in the experts. Those would be people who install television and radio equipment. They will have experience running cables and wires in all sorts of different situations.

Last but not least, don't overlook good lighting. This is a radio shack, not a cave. Make sure you have good task lighting for your work area as well as enough light in the rest of the room to prevent you from tripping over cords. A window where you can bring in natural lighting during the day would be a huge bonus.

Chapter 4
ONLINE COMMUNICATION

If phone lines are jammed and text messages don't seem to be getting through, another approach you could take is to utilize one or more online resources. Not only might these tools be available to you when everything else has failed, you can use them anywhere you can find a computer with online access, such as a library.

Even if your normal phone service isn't working, your smartphone should be able to glom onto any available Wi-Fi signals. Same thing goes for your tablets and other devices. Many businesses have backup generators and other preparations in place so as to keep functioning during emergencies. Those safeguards likely include ways to keep their Internet working. Position yourself close enough to the building, and you can probably pick up the signal. Fingers crossed they have at least one publicly available Wi-Fi channel. Remember, the point here is to have many options available to you when the chips are down.

INSTANT MESSAGING

With the prevalence of texting today, you may sometimes forget about standalone apps or websites that allow for instant messaging (IM). As I go through a few of these options, keep in mind that they will only work if you and the person with whom you are trying to communicate have the same programs or apps available. Most IM apps utilize some sort of notification to alert the recipient of an incoming message, so you need not be actively monitoring the airwaves, so to speak. But you do need to have the app installed and up and running.

Another thing to keep in mind is that while these programs and apps are free, at least at the time of this writing, they are also worth every glitch you may experience from time to time. Consider IM only as a backup to your other methods of emergency communication.

One example of this sort of IM app is Kik. It is a free app you can download and install on your smartphone (Kik.com). It works very much like texting but utilizes your Internet connection to operate. This is an excellent option for those who purchase prepaid cell phones and would rather save their texting minutes for emergencies. Note, however, that at the time of this writing, this is pretty much a mobile-only solution, meaning you won't be able to use it from a desktop or laptop computer, only your smartphone. Still, though, if you're able to get online with your phone, it is an option.

Skype is one of the oldest IM programs still available today. Many people are familiar with the video chat capability of Skype. You can use it as an IM program on desktops as well as mobile devices. A quick and free download is available on Skype.com. I've found the quality of calls and video varies based on the strength of the Internet signal. But, again, it is free and when you have a strong signal, the quality rivals anything else you put against it, paid service or not.

ONLINE IS FOREVER

If it is posted online, it is available, at least in some form, forever. This is an immutable fact, along the lines of water is wet and the sky is blue. It might not be accessible to *you*, but someone properly motivated and with the right skills and tools will be able to find it. I have personally been able to retrieve images and social media posts people thought were long since deleted or erased. And, honestly, I'm nowhere near as skilled as, say, a tabloid journalist with a tight deadline. Think twice, and then think again, before posting that photo online.

Not only are images available forever, those taken with modern technology can contain metadata, which is basically information hidden inside the image. This data might include the date and time the photo was taken, along with the camera's GPS coordinates when the photo was snapped. Savvy tech users could use that information to come right to your doorstep. Verexif.com is one site that will not only show you the information available in the metadata, but remove it so you can safely post the photo online.

Facebook Messenger has been around for a while now, and I'd bet most of the people on your contact list already have it installed on their phones. You can use it on desktops and laptops, too, simply by sending messages via Facebook chat. Download the app at Messenger.com. There have been, and likely will always be, some concerns about Facebook spying on its users. If this worries you but you want to have this IM program as an option, you could always set up dummy Facebook accounts and use them only for this purpose.

EMAIL

I know, email seems almost quaint nowadays, akin to handwriting letters and using actual stamps to send them through the mail. Even so, a quick email could help calm fears about your possible demise in the wake of a disaster. There are a ton of free email providers on the Web, such as Gmail and Yahoo. Many of them have corresponding apps for smartphones and tablets, too.

I recommend choosing two providers and setting up accounts on each for every member of your family or group. This way, if one provider isn't available due to the nature of the disaster or some other reason, you can use the other as a backup. You might also want to set up an email distribution list in each email account's contact list. This way, it is just a matter of sending one short email message to a single contact in the list and it will be sent out to everyone automatically.

TWITTER

One of numerous social media sites and apps out there, Twitter is unique in that it limits messages to 140 characters. For our purposes, that's not necessarily a bad thing. We all have that one person in our group who can't seem to be quick and concise with their communication, right? If you're not sure who in your group that is, most likely it is you. You'll find Twitter on the Internet at Twitter.com, and there is an app for it as well. Once you have it installed, make sure each member of your group is following every other member, which isn't nearly as complicated as it sounds. In addition to broadcasting messages to all of your followers, Twitter also has a direct message feature if you need to keep something relatively private. You can also tag a specific user in your message to help ensure they see it.

FACEBOOK

I mentioned Facebook earlier when talking about their Messenger app. But as the reigning king of social media sites, it bears a separate listing. Facebook has grown from relatively humble roots into a juggernaut that seems unstoppable. While there are still individuals out there who have resisted signing up for an account, their numbers are infinitesimal compared to those who have been assimilated. Facebook is incredibly easy to use and, like every other site and app in this chapter, is free. However, it isn't perfect. For example, Facebook will sometimes limit your reach, meaning a message you post might not be seen by everyone on your friend list. There have also been many reports of difficulty with keeping things private on Facebook. Again, social media sites like Facebook are worth every inconvenience we pay to use them.

One interesting feature Facebook offers that might be of interest is the use of groups. Facebook users can create private groups and either invite or directly add friends to them. Once the group is created and the privacy settings adjusted, anything posted in the group is visible only to the other members, at least in theory. This might be an excellent option for a means of keeping everyone in your group on the same page, so to speak, with emergency notifications. With the settings adjusted properly, Facebook will notify the user of new posts to the group.

OTHER SOCIAL MEDIA SITES

There are a ton of other social media sites out there, with more being created every day, all vying to be the next Facebook and earn the creators untold riches. Fads and popularity come and go and in the online world, it happens at light speed. If you find a site that seems to work particularly well for your needs, have at it. Just be aware that any website could disappear overnight, no matter how popular it may be. In fact, the more traffic and attention the site receives, the more often it might be seen as a target of interest for hackers.

Currently, popular social media sites include Instagram and Pinterest, neither of which are truly of interest when it comes to rapid communication during an emergency. But that's not to say the next big thing won't be useful for our purposes. Time will tell. Best to keep an ear to the ground, or at least pay attention to what's trending.

MESSAGE BOARDS

If email is seen as antiquated, message boards are positively prehistoric. Descendants of the Bulletin Board System (BBS) that populated what once passed for the online world, message boards are still in use, though they aren't nearly as popular as they were even five years ago. Often, message boards are centered on a specific community, hobby, or interest. They are typically part of a larger website devoted to the topic at hand, such as a specific TV show or a manufacturer.

A message board could be an excellent way for members of your group to keep in touch, particularly if the disaster is regional or larger, and the group members are scattered to the four winds. You'll need to create a website and install the message board onto it, but the average nine-year-old can handle that for you if need be. Name the site and the board something innocuous if you fear someone stumbling on it, though most message boards can be set with fairly tight privacy.

BLOGS

I don't know that I'd recommend using a blog for the primary purpose of emergency communication, but it could certainly be used to transmit messages in a pinch. A blog really isn't suited for two-way communication, other than perhaps trading comments back and forth. However, if you need to reach a lot of people quickly, that's easily done by posting a quick message on the blog, provided that those you want to reach either subscribe to blog updates or know to watch the blog for new posts. WordPress.com is one of the most popular, free blog platforms today.

INFORMATION PROVIDERS

Once upon a time, the Internet was referred to as the information superhighway. While that term may have fallen out of favor around the time AOL stopped sending out free disks to every household in America about every eight days or so, the sentiment remains the same. While up until now, this chapter has been focused on methods of online, two-way communication, I'd be remiss not to mention using the Internet to gather information during and after disaster strikes.

There are, of course, a bazillion different news sites out there, some more reliable than others, but all with their own bias and slant on the news. Long gone are the days of reporters simply sharing the vetted information or their own personal eyewitness account of an event. Today, it is all about who can get there first and who can report the newest information, regardless of how true it might turn out to be in the end. With that in mind, no matter which news sites you decide to monitor, take the initial reports with a grain of salt. They are likely to be full of conjectures and half-truths.

With regard to news sites, I recommend monitoring a few now and deciding how reliable you find them as time goes on. If a site seems to get as much information wrong as it does right, you may want to consider a different information provider. Choosing a news site is, believe it or not, a rather personal decision. Each site is going to be different in terms of not only the stories it shares, but how the information is provided, from a "just the facts, ma'am" approach to one that is far more entertaining.

Don't overlook sites that are based in other countries, either. Often, news agencies from overseas will be free of the politics that often determine what and how news is reported in the United States. Plus, reporters at the BBC always sound so calm and composed, no matter how outlandish the story they are reporting.

I suggest choosing at least three different news agencies to bookmark for monitoring during or after a disaster strikes. One local, one regional, and one national station, at a minimum. This way, you'll hopefully be covered no matter how large or small the affected area may be.

You should also choose one or two weather-reporting websites because even if the disaster at hand isn't related to Mother Nature, she's sure to put her own spin on things at some point or another. As with the news agencies, pick a couple and monitor them for a while to see how reliable they are, then go from there.

The online world is chock-full of websites, apps, and pro-grams that are designed for rapid communication. It would be folly to ignore these potential tools. However, the Internet is just as subject to disaster as anything else. Hackers can take sites down, power failures can take servers offline. As with everything else in this book, though, it's still a good idea to be aware of the various options that are available to you.

Chapter 5

PUTTING A PLAN TOGETHER

There are three main purposes behind emergency communication. First and foremost, you want to ensure the safety and security of each person in your family or group. When disaster hits, your initial first concern outside of keeping yourself alive is making sure your loved ones make it through the storm, so to speak.

Once you've done that, the second purpose comes into play, which is to determine the next plan of action. In many situations, that might be as simple as everyone getting together at home. In other cases, it might mean rallying at a secondary location or even traveling in separate caravans to a distant bug out spot.

The third objective of emergency communication is information gathering. This actually serves the first two purposes when you get right down to it. The more information you can obtain about the situation at hand, the more effectively you'll be able to keep you and your family safe as well as plan the next course of action.

PLAN BASICS

Your emergency communication plan needs to cover a few basic elements.

- With whom will you need to communicate?
- What method(s) will you use to communicate with them?
- When will you communicate with them? How often?

The "who" is easy. Your immediate family as well as those in your survival group will be among the first you'll want to contact. Anyone beyond that level will depend on the nature and extent of the disaster. If you have a sufficiently large or complicated network, you might need to reach out to emergency services for assistance.

What methods will you use to communicate? Well, I just spent several chapters covering those, didn't I? Pick the methods that work for you and that fit into your overall preparedness plans. Always veer toward the tools with which you have had regular practice to ensure competency.

The schedule for communication is critical and absolutely must be understood by all involved. Here's the thing: Depending on the circumstances, it might not be in your best interest to have your phone ring or your radio go off without warning. Therefore, a schedule of some sort should be devised and agreed upon ahead of time.

Set up a schedule for those who are mobile to attempt contact with those who are at home once every hour. Determine in advance when the attempts are to take place, such as at half past every hour. If you have multiple family or group members who are likely to be away from home when disaster hits, consider scheduling each of their calls at a different time. For example, Dad is to call at the top of the hour, Mom is to call at a quarter past, the 16-year-old at half past, and so on. This should help eliminate the possibility of being busy with one person when another is trying to call in.

With all of that said, the initial attempt at contact should be as soon as possible after disaster hits. It is important to touch base with all involved to ensure their safety and then to determine the next course of action.

PACE

PACE is an acronym often used when setting up a communication plan. The acronym is applicable across the board when talking about disaster readiness, but the focus here is obviously on communication. Essentially, PACE is a four-stage methodology for planning.

P = Primary

A = Alternate

C = Contingency

E = Emergency

(P) This represents the first communication plan to use. This should be the method that is most likely to succeed on the first attempt as well as the easiest for all to use.

(A) If the primary means of communication isn't working, this is your backup plan. Ideally, it will be almost as good as your primary method in terms of both ease of use and likelihood of success.

(C) If both primary and alternate methods aren't working, this is where you'll turn. While you'd hope the first two methods would be successful, you need to plan for the possibility that they won't be.

(E) If all else fails, this is what you'll do. This is the last resort, when all bets are off and you're desperately trying to get in touch with someone.

For each person in your family or group, you should go through the PACE process and determine the means of communication for each level. Doing so will help you figure out the details of your overall emergency communication plan. To clarify, what we're determining is how you or whoever is nominally in charge of the family will reach out to each person. Here's how it works.

Contact: Michael (son, age 13)

P = Text message

A = Phone call

C = Email to Gmail account

E = Depending on the circumstance, either drive to school for face-to-face communication, or leave a note at home.

The Emergency component is always a last resort where the odds for success might be questionable, but it is still better than nothing. In this case, Michael has been instructed to hunker down at school until a parent arrives in the event of a major crisis. If school isn't safe, he's to head for home along a specific route so his parents can watch for him and vice versa. When he arrives home, if no one else is there, he's to look for a note in a specific location to let him know what to do.

Here's another example:

Contact: Alan (amateur radio contact)

P = Ham radio

A = Text message

C = Phone call

E = Email

Odds are if a ham operator isn't responding via radio, text, or phone, something catastrophic has happened on their end. Sending an email allows for the message to be seen at a later date. For example, imagine that Alan had to evacuate due to damage to his home. Once he reached his own bug out location, he'd likely boot up a laptop or tablet and use email to get in touch with family.

PACE is just one more tool for planning your emergency communication strategy, nothing more. If it works for you, great. If not, find something else that does.

CRISIS COMMUNICATIONS HUB

Part of your overall communication plan should involve setting up a crisis communications hub to be contacted in the immediate aftermath of a disaster. This person will serve as a backup to your attempts to contact family members directly.

The goal here has little to do with long-term communications. Rather, it is to rally the troops and ensure everyone in your immediate tribe is safe and secure. To do that, you'll need to enlist the help of someone you trust who doesn't live in your local area. For the purposes of this discussion, I'll concentrate on local or regional emergencies and nothing on the scale of nuclear war or an electromagnetic pulse (EMP).

The person you select to be your communications hub should be reliable and familiar with several forms of communication, such as texting, email, and perhaps even ham radio. They should also be generally Internet savvy and have strong Google search skills. In other words, Aunt Sally might not be the best choice if she is the one constantly calling you to fix her computer because she keeps winning the Nigerian lottery.

The communications hub needs to live outside of your immediate area to help ensure they won't be directly affected by the disaster affecting you. You don't want your hub to live just down the street or even in the next town. Instead, look for someone who is perhaps out of state. It should go without saying that you'll need to have a discussion with this person and obtain their agreement to act as the communications hub, and you should offer to do the same for them. Never expect someone to commit to something you're not willing to do for them in return.

The communications hub has a couple of different responsibilities. First and foremost, they receive messages from scattered family members if they are unable to make contact directly with one another.

Example: A disaster hits while Bobby is in school and his parents are at work. His mom is unable to reach Bobby by cell phone. Bobby finds out he can't use his cell phone to make calls. Following the emergency communication protocol his family set up, he immediately logs on to his laptop and sends an email to their crisis communications hub, Uncle Chris. When his mom calls Chris for an update, he's able to tell her that Bobby is fine and plans to wait at his school until she picks him up.

The second function of the communications hub is to conduct research and gather information about the situation.

Access to the Internet and other resources might be limited or nonexistent for those in the thick of a disaster. Having someone outside the affected area who can pass along news reports or maybe even help direct emergency workers to your area could be critical. If your chosen communications hub isn't as proficient with online searching as you'd like, you could start by setting up a bookmark folder on their computer with all of the major national and local news agencies and other sites listed and ready to go.

THE 3-3-3 RADIO PLAN

I found this idea on a website and thought it was a great. I've tweaked it a bit before including it here. If you know who originated the 3-3-3 Radio Plan, please send them my way so I can thank them personally and include proper attribution in a later edition.

The 3-3-3 plan isn't necessarily the best approach for communicating with immediate family or close group members. A combination of information gathering and social networking, it is more for touching base with people who might be in your area and beyond.

The idea behind the 3-3-3 plan is to provide for some consistency with regard to long-term emergency communication. Having a formalized structure reduces the amount of blind luck it might take to get in touch with someone else when telephones are out of operation. My understanding is that the 3-3-3 plan is also a spin on all of the different Rules of Three that preppers have developed or quoted over the years. These include:

> *"Three is two, two is one, and one is none when it comes to critical pieces of gear."*

and

> *"You can survive three minutes without air, three hours without shelter, three days without water, and three weeks without food."*

In a nutshell, the 3-3-3 plan says to turn on your radio every three hours, tune it to channel 3, and leave it on for three full minutes. Like most things in life, though, it is a bit more complicated than it seems on the surface.

Timing

The plan states to turn on the radio every three hours. Remember, the whole idea here is to achieve some sort of common ground with regard to a schedule. So, beginning at 12:00 a.m., turn on the radio every three hours:

12:00 a.m.	12:00 p.m.
3:00 a.m.	3:00 p.m.
6:00 a.m.	6:00 p.m.
9:00 a.m.	9:00 p.m.

The times given are local. However, if you live very near a time zone border, you might consider doubling up your monitoring time to cover both zones, at least during the times when you are most likely to make contact with another station, such as morning and evening.

While you might not realistically be able to monitor the early-morning hours every day, it might be worth your while to check out the midnight and 3:00 a.m. times once in a while. During those times, the sun won't affect radio waves in your area, allowing you to potentially tune in broadcasts from much farther away.

Of course, if all anyone did was listen and they never broadcasted anything, you could have a hundred people in the area all thinking they are the last ones alive. Take a couple of seconds to send out a quick message in an attempt to make contact with others. It need not be elaborate or revealing. Just mention your call sign and send a request for contact from anyone listening.

Channel

According to the 3-3-3 plan, you are to tune your radio to channel 3. Now, that works okay when we're talking about radios that have a channel 3, such as CB and FRS/GMRS devices. But what about ham radios? Well, one of the reasons why it is important to obtain your ham license and practice with the equipment in advance of an emergency is to make contact with other ham operators in your area. Determine the most common broadcast frequencies being used, and when it comes time to implement the 3-3-3 plan, concentrate on those.

You might go so far as to make plans with some of those other ham operators, getting them on board with the 3-3-3 plan and specifying certain frequencies to use when the plan is put into operation.

Duration

The plan states to leave your radio on for a full three minutes. As a matter of course, I'd extend that to at least five minutes, preferably even longer if you have sufficient power. The reason is even if you are in sync with the atomic clock and have the exact time down to the millisecond, others might not. Give them the benefit of the doubt and work some extra monitoring time into your plan, if possible.

Some advocate for extending the monitoring for as long as 15 minutes. That's great, if you have the power to sustain that schedule for days or weeks on end.

The whole point of the 3-3-3 plan is to set out some sort of agreed-upon schedule to make it easier to communicate with other radio operators during a crisis. Sure, you might get lucky and randomly find someone transmitting at any given time of day or night. But the 3-3-3 plan takes the guesswork out of the equation. If you plan to implement the 3-3-3 plan, talk to people in your area now and get them on board as well.

THE 3-2-1 RADIO PLAN

I can't say with certainty which came first, the 3-3-3 plan or the 3-2-1 plan. In practice, they are very similar. The

3-2-1 plan appears to have originally been developed by the American Redoubt Radio Operators Network (AmRRON).

The "3" refers to the channel. As with the 3-3-3 plan, you are to use channel 3 on your FRS/GMRS or CB radio. The "2" signifies the duration of your broadcast and monitoring. You are to keep your radio on for at least two minutes. The "1" is for the timing, every hour on the hour.

The reality is that it truly doesn't matter which plan you use, so long as all in your group are aware of the choice and agree to follow it. Naturally, you're welcome to come up with your own variation, one that is particularly well suited for your group's needs. The important part of this is to make a plan and stick with it.

BUG OUT COMMUNICATIONS

Having the ability to stay in contact with family members or others who are bugging out with you is critical. Some members of the party may become separated, either by accident or design. You may need to call for help, assuming there is help to be had from someone. If nothing else, you'll want to be able to listen to radio broadcasts to stay up to speed on the situation at hand. While our omnipresent cell phones are typically going to be our primary means of communication, if the cell networks are overwhelmed or nonexistent, you'll want to have other options available.

Of course, bugging out means you won't have ready access to an AC outlet. You need to think portable. This means batteries and/or alternate sources of power.

If your primary concern is gathering information, a standard emergency radio that runs on either batteries or crank power will suffice. Most of the ones sold today will tune in AM/FM and NOAA weather broadcasts. Some of the nicer ones will also bring in shortwave transmissions. The Kaito Voyager Pro is one of the best on the market today and will handle all of those transmissions, plus it adds solar power to the mix.

Baofeng UV-5R Ham Radio

This transmitter is very popular among preppers for its small size and inexpensive price. It is an excellent option for the bug out bag as well as for home use.

For two-way communication, it is hard to beat a small handheld ham transmitter/receiver, or transceiver. The Baofeng UV-5R is very popular among preppers due to the small size and wide range of capabilities. It takes some effort to get it programmed properly, though. My advice is to invest in the proper programming cable so you can program the radio using a free downloadable program called CHIRP.

Be sure to keep spare batteries in your bug out bag, ideally one full set for each radio or other device you'll be carrying. You might also consider picking up a portable solar panel. They have really come down in price recently and are rather affordable. Many of them fold up into a size not much larger than a spiral notebook, though around an inch or two thick. You can use the solar panel to charge not only your cell phone or tablet but a set of batteries, too.

EXPECT IT TO BE COMPLICATED

When I was in school, one of the only computer languages being taught at the middle and high school levels was BASIC, which stands for Beginner's All-Purpose Symbolic Instruction Code. It was, well, pretty basic in that much of it was written in very simple terms. The instruction to print, for example, was "Print." One of the first types of commands you learn in BASIC is the conditional "If/Then" statement. Basically (no pun intended), if a specified condition were true, then the program performed a certain action. If the condition were not true, the program moved to the next step or sequence.

Your communication plan is going to be filled with If/Then conditional statements, even if they aren't written in that format. For example:

IF Dad can't be reached by telephone at work,
THEN send him a text.

IF text messages aren't going through or there is no response,
THEN send him an email.

Obviously, this can get complicated quickly. That's okay, and really, it is to be expected. There's no way around it. As you acquire more and more means to communicate, there will be ever more steps in the communication plan. The PACE protocol alone specifies four distinct steps in the process, each of them very much If/Then conditions.

Complicated isn't necessarily bad, provided you take the time to fully understand each step in the plan and ensure all involved know the parts they will play.

A SAMPLE PLAN

Let me put it all together to demonstrate how this works with the fictional Branson family.

Ron: Father of Todd and Eddie; husband of Susan. Works in the city about 40 miles from home. Each morning, he drives to the train station about 10 miles away, then takes the train into the city.

Susan: Mother of Todd and Eddie; wife of Ron. Works from home as a web designer. Occasionally, she travels locally to meet with new and current clients but is rarely more than 20 miles from home.

Todd: 16-year-old sophomore attending school about seven miles from home.

Eddie: 14-year-old eighth grader attending school one block away from Todd's high school.

In this situation, Susan is home most of the time so she'll serve as the linchpin for the overall communication plan.

As a family, they've discussed the various possible and likely scenarios that could affect their area.

Over the years, they've discovered that Ron's cell service while at work is spotty at best. It doesn't seem to matter which provider they use, there's just something about the building where his office is located that muddies the signal. Interestingly enough, if someone leaves him a voice mail, the alert for it comes through just fine. With that in mind, his PACE looks like this:

Contact: Ron

Primary: Call office landline.

Alternate: Call cell phone and leave a message if he doesn't answer.

Contingency: Send a text message.

Emergency: Send an email.

When Todd and Eddie are in school, their cell phones are to be turned off according to the rules. The PACE for both of them takes that into account by utilizing their student email accounts first:

Contacts: Todd and Eddie

Primary: Email student email account.

Alternate: Send a text message.

Contingency: Call cell phone, leaving a voice mail if there is no answer.

Emergency: Call school office and leave a message there.

In this case, let's say a terrorist-related bombing occurred in the city at 12:45 p.m. Susan, who always has a radio tuned to a local oldies station while working, hears about the bombing when a newscaster interrupts the broadcast with the breaking story.

The first step in their emergency communication plan after a disaster in or near the city is for Susan to try to reach Ron if he's at work. Susan tries calling Ron at his office (Primary) but gets a fast busy signal. Calls to his cell (Alternate) go immediately to voice mail. She leaves him a message asking him to call home or to call her cell right away. She fires off a text message (Contingency) to him as well, but gets no immediate response. Finally, she uses her tablet to send him an email (Emergency). Having satisfied all four PACE elements in the span of a few minutes, Susan moves on to reaching out to the kids. Naturally, if the crisis were more localized, Susan would have reversed the order and concentrated on the children first.

Susan immediately hears back from both Todd and Eddie, who each received their mother's email. Todd says the news is spreading through the high school like wildfire and there are already rumors that students will be let out early. Eddie hadn't heard about the bombing and is concerned about his dad. Susan instructs both of them to turn on their cell phones but to keep them on silent. She wants to be able to contact them immediately should the need arise. She also tells them to stay put until and unless school is let out early. If that happens, they are to let her know right away as the school district's communication procedures are sometimes lacking.

Susan then reaches out to the family's communications hub, her brother-in-law Brian. He lives a few hundred miles away and since taking early retirement, he's become quite a news junkie. She sends him a quick email asking if he has any information on the situation in the city and follows the email with a text message letting him know to check his inbox. She hears back almost instantly, but learns that he hasn't heard anything she doesn't already know from listening to the radio and watching TV.

Also, Brian has not heard from Ron as of yet, which is troubling. Brian promises to notify her immediately if or when that changes.

Susan then goes into their home office and turns on the ham radio equipment. Their fallback position on emergency communication is to attempt to reach Ron via radio. He carries a small radio transceiver (a single unit that both transmits and receives) in his bug out bag. Just as she's beginning to tune to the proper frequency, her cell phone pings with a new text message. She doesn't recognize the number, but the message reads:

"This is Ron. Lost my phone and am using Joe's. Caught a ride with him and heading south out of town. Phone calls won't get through. Will advise when we reach my car. ETA to train lot 45 min. Love you."

Joe, she recalls, is one of Ron's coworkers. She's never met him but says a silent prayer of thanks that he's helped Ron find a way out of the city. She then sends a text message to Todd and Eddie to let them know their father is safe and on the way home.

Going online with her laptop, Susan begins monitoring one of the police scanner websites they have bookmarked for such a situation. Using that site, along with Google Maps, she's able to figure out where roads are being closed and rerouted, information she sends back to Ron via text message. This allows Ron and Joe to avoid the worst of the traffic snarls, getting Ron to his car, and finally, home, much quicker.

Every communication plan is going to look different. Each family or group comes to the table with their own needs. The first plan you devise isn't likely to be perfect, either. You need to take the time to test out different scenarios and even run some drills to tweak things here and there. The important thing is to get the ball rolling now and start putting your plan together today.

Chapter 6

EMERGENCY BUSINESS COMMUNICATIONS PLANNING

Like individuals and families, businesses need to plan for how they will communicate before, during, and after a crisis. Even if you're not a business owner yourself, I encourage you to read this chapter carefully. Many businesses today still lack proper emergency planning protocols. Talk to the management where you work and find out what plans they have in the books. If they shrug their shoulders and say they haven't gotten around to it yet, consider lending them your copy of this book.

Keep in mind that the emergency might be limited to the business itself. It could be something relatively minor, such as a plumbing issue that cuts off water to the building for a day or two. Or, it could be something far greater, like a gas fire. In either case, there are several different categories of people who need to be considered for emergency communications planning.

MANAGEMENT

Any members of management not already on site when the crisis occurs need to be notified immediately. Their contact information, including cell phone and email address, should be readily accessible for such emergencies. The information doesn't need to be posted in the employee lounge, of course, but it shouldn't require three sets of keys and seven different passwords either. Have it posted or available in a supervisor's office and ensure there are always two different employees on staff at any time who can access the information when needed. This way, should something happen to the first person, there is a backup available.

Of course, not all emergencies require the presence of every member of senior management. But, as a general rule of thumb, it is better to err on the side of caution and send out a notification when it might be unnecessary than to have one of your vice presidents first learn about the crisis on CNN.

EMPLOYEES

I've always believed that employees are any company's most valuable asset. Without those punching the clock day in and day out, the company doesn't function. Employee safety is, or should be, paramount to any emergency plan.

In many companies, human resources (HR) is the primary liaison between the company and the employee. The HR department handles everything, from benefits to time clock issues. HR also typically maintains all employee files, which include contact information for each of them. Most HR personnel are also trained to handle sensitive issues. HR staff members know the importance of confidentiality, which can be vitally important when dealing with outside agencies as well as the media.

Because of all of this, HR is in an ideal position to coordinate the communications between the company and employees. In fact, the HR department could truly be the emergency communications hub for the company as a whole.

There needs to be a plan in place for notifying employees en masse during non-working hours, should the need arise. This could be a message sent out via email and text or, if the company is fairly small, a series of phone calls might suffice. While the company won't likely reach every single employee, the more who are notified quickly, the better. The grapevine will surely come into play as well, with employees calling or texting one another.

Whether this responsibility is assigned to HR or to another person or department, it needs to be crystal clear who is handling it.

Additionally, consider the possibility that disaster could strike during working hours. The overall emergency response plan should include evacuation procedures as well as instructions for sheltering in place. Naturally, these procedures and instructions should include how best to notify the employees who are present at the time of the crisis. If the company is small, this could be as simple as the supervisor walking around and speaking with each employee individually or talking to them in small groups.

Larger organizations might find it easier to gather all employees into one area, such as the break room or a meeting room, to discuss the situation. Most large factories as well as offices have some sort of intercom or speaker system that can be utilized to make a mass announcement.

No matter how large or small the company, it is vitally important that great care be taken to avoid panic. Stick to the facts of the situation and avoid gossip and rumors. Having a solid plan in place ahead of time and sharing that plan with the employees will go a long way toward keeping people calm.

If feasible, run periodic drills with the employees so each knows their responsibility should a disaster strike. Fire drills are commonplace, of course, but how about tornado or earthquake drills?

CUSTOMERS

If the business routinely has customers on site, such as a retail store, inform those people immediately if the business is closing due to the emergency. Don't assume that the nature of the crisis will make that obvious. I can tell you from experience that some people just don't have the common sense of a peanut butter sandwich and will venture out in the nastiest conditions for the most inane reasons.

If the nature of the crisis doesn't allow for phone calls to be answered at the business location, set up an outgoing message informing callers that, at the minimum, the business is closed temporarily due to the emergency at hand. A better solution, though perhaps not practical in all situations, would be to have calls rerouted to a secondary location staffed by a few employees who can assure callers that the delay in business is only temporary as well as answer questions to the best of their ability. This would be an excellent job for an experienced sales staff.

Someone in the company should be in charge of updating the website or blog as well. Post a simple message letting people know that the business is closed for a bit but will reopen shortly. As the situation develops, the website or blog will be a great tool to keep people updated. If the company maintains any sort of online mailing list, utilize that as well.

SUPPLIERS/VENDORS

If there are deliveries scheduled for the day, alert affected vendors or suppliers to the situation. Part of the goal of the emergency business communications plan is to limit the traffic coming and going from the business. For every vendor you're able to contact and cancel, that's one less person and vehicle that will have to be turned away upon arrival.

NEWS MEDIA

If the crisis is of sufficient magnitude, you may be visited or called by members of the media. A very clear company policy should be in place authorizing specific spokespersons to address news agencies and the like. It is far better for the company to present one individual who is not only well-informed, but trained to handle media inquiries. While many people are looking for their own 15 minutes of fame, it shouldn't come at the company's expense.

Keep in mind that no privately held company has a legal obligation to speak to any news agency. It might be best for all involved to just provide a "No comment" until more information about the situation is known.

That said, always tell the truth about what happened. I'm not suggesting you play every card in your hand, but be very careful with the media. If you lie or try to cover up facts and are caught, the company will most likely be raked over the coals.

GOVERNMENT AGENCIES

Depending upon the nature of the emergency, one or more government agencies may respond. It is absolutely critical that the company fully cooperate with the agencies involved in recovery efforts, search and rescue, and the like. Just make the assumption that they know far more than HR about finding people who may be trapped in the building, and let them go to work.

As for regulatory agencies and those with similar responsibilities, well, that's why you want management notified as soon as possible. Let the suits make the decision on how to handle those people.

Whether the company has 5 employees or 5,000, a plan needs to be in place for how the company is going to communicate during and after a disaster. The plan should be in writing, shared with all employees, and stored as a hard copy somewhere on site so it can be referenced needed. A copy should also be stored electronically off site so it can be accessed online should the hard copy be barbecued in the crisis.

Chapter 7
CODES AND CIPHERS

When using any form of communication, it might be wise to apply some sort of code in order to keep your messages secure. While it might sound a bit silly, the reality is that anything you put on paper could theoretically be used against you if the wrong person discovers it. The same thing goes for verbal communication. Mankind has been using codes and ciphers for centuries to varying degrees of success.

CODES VERSUS CIPHERS

Throughout this chapter, I'll be using the word "code" as a general term to refer to methods of obscuring messages so they cannot be read or understood by those outside the community or group. However, there is a difference between codes and ciphers. Simply put, codes obscure the message by using entirely different words or phrases, where a cipher changes the individual letters within the intended message to keep it secret.

For example, let's say the intended message (called "plaintext" by the professionals) is DOG. A simple substitution cipher using the numeric equivalent of each letter (A=1, B=2, etc.) transforms the message into 4/15/7. A cipher results in a message the same length as the plaintext, unless the cipher's rules specifically state otherwise.

Here's one to decode on your own:

2/5 19/21/18/5 20/15 4/18/9/14/11 25/15/21/18 15/22/ 1/12/20/9/14/5.

A code, on the other hand, necessitates an agreed-upon understanding that the word for DOG is LAMP or some other equally innocuous word. Codes are often used to convey the simplest of messages, such as an order to attack or to retreat to a designated location. When the code is limited to that sort of use, an actual code book likely isn't necessary. I'll discuss this further later in the chapter.

CIPHERS

Many of us developed or learned some sort of substitution code when we were children. It was great fun to send secret messages to our friends, confident as we were in our abilities to outwit those who might try to break our ciphers.

Here are a couple of examples you might use today:

Simple Substitution Code

A	B	C	D	E	F	G	H	I	J	K	L	M
N	O	P	Q	R	S	T	U	V	W	X	Y	Z

When writing a message, simply substitute the letter above or below the correct one. For example, PREPPER becomes CERCCRE.

Another simple substitution code uses a matrix or graph.

Simple Substitution Matrix

	1	2	3	4	5
A	A	B	C	D	E
B	F	G	H	I	J
C	K	L	M	N	O
D	P	Q	R	S	T
E	U	V	W	X	Y/Z

To use the matrix, substitute each letter with its coordinates, so that PREPPER becomes D1D3A5D1D1A5D3.

Once you've used these ciphers for a while, you'll start to memorize them. After some time, you won't need to have the table in front of you to write or read a message. Another nice feature is you don't necessarily need to have the table or chart squirreled away somewhere. When it comes time to write or read a message, it only takes a few seconds to write out the table for reference. When you're done, that scrap of paper can be destroyed.

The downside, though, is these ciphers are rather easy to break. There are very few one- or two-letter words in the

English language, so that is always a good place to start. Vowels and double letters are often easy to sort out, and the rest usually falls into place shortly after.

One way you can make things more difficult for the code breaker is to add unnecessary letters. For example, the coded message is always written such that the first and last letter of every word is gibberish or random. So, using our first code, PREPPER might become JCERCCREW. Writing a full sentence using Simple Substitution Code above would look like this:

I have seen the enemy and he is us. = HVK LUNIRF WFRRAU IGURC CRARZLJ ONAQW KURN PVFU YHFE.

With a lack of obvious one- and two-letter words, the breaker's job has become much tougher. You can play around with this basic idea, too, and change things up. For example, instead of adding random letters to the front and back of words, add them as the second and fourth letters or something else along those lines. As long as the person with whom you are communicating is on the same page as you, all should work fine.

CODE WORDS AND PHRASES

Another version of coded communication is to set up actual code words and phrases. While seemingly meaningless to the uninformed, the words or phrases have very distinct meanings to those on the receiving end, as with the following examples:

The chair is against the wall. = We are low on supplies.

John has a long mustache. = All is well on our end.

I've seen *Red Dawn* far too many times. = We need to set up a face-to-face meeting.

You might designate specific colors with certain meanings. For example, any sentence with the word "red" in it could mean your party needs help. "There was a red color to the sky this morning" would mean the same thing as "Why did bullfighters always use red capes?" Any time a color is used, the rest of the sentence can be disregarded and the recipient is to concentrate on just the agreed-upon meaning of the color.

It would probably be best to keep the number of code words and phrases to a minimum. The alternative is to create a code book, which is both cumbersome and a security risk. Instead, focus on about a dozen specific messages that would be important to communicate and then come up with codes for them.

USE OF FOREIGN OR INVENTED LANGUAGES

During World War II, the United States made use of Navajo code talkers to facilitate coded or secret communications. The Navajo language is incredibly complex and very few non-Navajos could speak it at the time. In 1942, at the outset of the program, a group of United States Marines who also happened to be Navajo gathered at Camp Pendleton in California to create a workable code based on their native language.

With a population as incredibly diverse that of the United States, even the smallest communities likely have members who are fluent or nearly so in more than one language. Of course, using a widely used language such as Spanish likely won't have the desired secrecy. Instead, look for individuals and families who know how to speak Haitian Creole, Latin, or other less familiar languages.

You have likely heard of, or perhaps are even fluent in, pig latin. This simple language game is popular among children. In pig latin, the first consonant sound of a word is moved to the end, then the sound "ay" is attached. So, the word "dog" would become "ogday." If the word begins with a vowel sound, "way" is tacked on, making "ever" into "everway." There are innumerable variations of this concept. When I was young, a group of my friends came up with one that inserted a "mum" sound between every syllable. Once you learn the rules and become familiar with it, understanding what is said is easy. To the outsider, though, it all sounds like gibberish.

CODED GESTURES AND VISUAL CUES

Codes might not utilize verbal or written communication. If members of your group go out on patrol or on scavenging missions, there should be some sort of protocol for when they return in order to ensure they haven't been compromised or aren't under duress. This need not be something overly complicated, such as a series of bird whistles with specific call and response patterns required in order for safe passage. That's pretty much just Hollywood nonsense and impractical out in the real world. After all, not everyone knows how to whistle, or is let alone capable of imitating the call of a Lady Gouldian finch on demand.

There are two very compelling reasons why spoken code words or phrases should be avoided for camp entry. First, they could be overheard and used by an attacking party trying to sneak into the camp. Second, people can be forgetful. It would be bad enough for the camp to end up on alert because a returning scout simply forgot the new code word, and that sort of system tends to cause laziness with the guards. They might hesitate to sound any sort of alarm in the future if it turned out to be all for nothing the last time.

Instead, your safeguard could be as simple as each member of the scout party being issued yellow bandannas. Upon their return to camp, if the bandannas are tied to the outside of their packs or hanging from their pants pockets, it would indicate something amiss, such as the belief that they are being followed. If this were to happen, the scout party would be allowed to enter camp and, at the same time, the guards placed on full alert.

A simple gesture could work, too. Rubbing the back of the neck, then moving the hand down the front of the chest to the belt buckle could indicate all is well. The opposite movement could mean the person is under duress.

The whole idea here is to be able to quickly and effectively communicate whether or not the returning party is safe and secure. You might consider setting up something so the guards can communicate a similar message to the returning party, conveying if all is well within the camp, but this might not be necessary. If all is not well, would the guards be present at the gate?

HIDDEN MESSAGES

Another component of keeping information away from those who may mean harm involves hiding the actual message in some way. One example of this is the dead drop. A dead drop involves leaving a written message in a pre-arranged hidden location, then utilizing some sort of signal to notify the intended recipient to look for the message. For example, the drop location might be behind a loose brick in the outer back wall of an abandoned building.

Here's how this might covertly play out:

> *I nonchalantly walk to the back of the building and, after checking carefully for possible surveillance, secure my written message behind the loose brick. I then*

leave the area and begin walking down the sidewalk. Approaching the third lightpost from the corner, I "accidentally" drop a pen. As I reach down to pick it up, I use a piece of chalk to make a small line at the base of the light post. Later that day or even the following week, my partner walks by the lightpost and looks for that mark. Seeing it, he knows there is a message waiting for him at the drop.

Sneaky? Yes. Kind of a pain in the butt? Absolutely. There's a lot of work involved with hiding and retrieving messages in this way. But, this sort of system has been used successfully for hundreds of years in one form or another. By the way, it is called a dead drop because there is no actual face-to-face interaction. If there were, it would be called a *live drop*.

One variation that immediately comes to mind is to utilize one of those fake rocks people buy for hiding a spare key near the front door. As I noted in my first book, *Prepper's Home Defense*, thieves looking to break in know to look for those, so don't use them for their intended purpose. But, you could easily use one for a dead drop. Just make sure to put it in a location not likely to be disturbed by construction and such.

Another interesting twist on the idea of hidden messages comes from the pop art world. A few years back, an artist named Aram Bartholl came up with a way to share computer files fairly anonymously. He began embedding USB flash drives into brick walls, leaving just the working end exposed. The project started in 2010 with five locations in New York City, then expanded to include over 1,500 locations around the world. Anyone can visit one of these sites and upload or download whatever files they wish. For those interested in seeing this art project up close and personal, visit DeadDrops.com. Bear in mind, though, that downloading random files from an anonymous flash drive is probably not the best decision you'll ever make. However, if the technology is still available at the time you need to send or receive covert messages, hiding a USB flash drive in a location of your choice might be a viable option.

The use of codes, ciphers, and other means of keeping your messages safe and secure is an important consideration. Such things are often considered as being more in the realm of secret agents and government snoops, but in reality, we all likely have information we'll want to keep secret and reveal to only a chosen few.

Concentrate on methods that are fairly simple and easy to remember. If the codes or ciphers are too complicated, people will either not remember how they work or they'll forgo using them out of laziness. That said, given that the point of using codes is to prevent others from discovering the true message, you probably want to avoid making them *too* simple.

Chapter 8

ESSENTIALS FOR EFFECTIVE COMMUNICATION

The tools of communication, from radios to smartphones, will only get you so far. You need to develop your communication *skills*, too. Think of it in terms of a firearm. While anyone can pull a trigger, you need practice in order to hit the target. The same thing applies here. Anyone can shoot their mouth off at someone, but it takes practice to get the point across.

In this chapter, I will touch upon several suggestions to help improve your interpersonal communication. While some readers may already have been doing what I suggest for years, others might notice a lightbulb go on above their heads.

In the last decade or so, our society's communication styles have changed distinctly. In large part, gone are the days of long, rambling telephone conversations with friends or sending handwritten letters to those who live far away. Instead, we often behave as though communicating with others, particularly verbally, is a distasteful chore, one we'd like to finish as soon as possible and with as little effort as we can muster. In fact, if we actually have to make a phone call and speak with someone, we are annoyed. Why couldn't we just send an email or text and be done with it? Talking takes too much time!

Because of this shift, many of us have lost what you might call conversational skills. You could even argue that younger generations never had them to lose. It's a capability that could turn out to be crucial at some point down the road. In the event of a prolonged disaster, the days of email and text will fall to the wayside. We'll actually have to, *gulp*, talk to one another.

Everything in this chapter can be used to improve your communication skills today. Most of these suggestions and techniques are geared toward face-to-face conversations. As such, these are things you'll use when talking with family members, friends, and coworkers, rather than in dealing with outsiders trying to negotiate entrance into your camp eight months after an EMP wiped out most technology.

In other words, you're far more likely to make genuine use of this information than you are knowing how to build a Faraday cage out of a metal garbage can, though that knowledge may indeed prove useful someday.

AVOID DISTRACTIONS

This is one of the simplest ways to improve communication, yet it can also be one of the most difficult things for many people to do. Think back—when was the last time you maintained eye contact while talking to your spouse or one of your children? Odds are, most of the time, you aren't giving the other person your complete, undivided attention. You're checking your phone, cooking dinner, paging through the newspaper, or doing one of another thousand other things while talking. Not only can this lead to misunderstandings because you only hear part of what is being said, the other person can develop feelings of resentment and anger because they feel, rightly so in many cases, that you're placing a higher priority on Facebook than you are in speaking with them directly.

Put down the mobile devices and maintain eye contact. This tells the person you feel what they have to say is important, and they'll feel more comfortable speaking with you. Plus, you'll be able to tune in to body language a lot more easily if you're actually watching the person speak. I'm not saying you need to turn off the TV, square your shoulders, and stare deep into their eyes every time your loved one wants to talk to you. But if he or she says, "We need to talk," you're best off putting social media on hold for a bit.

One last thing to remember: There's a fine line between maintaining proper eye contact and staring with the intensity of a serial killer. In some instances, the latter may prove useful, too.

ACTIVE LISTENING

One of the most critical elements of good communication is to actually listen to the other person and work to understand what they are truly saying to you. All too often, when we're in a heated discussion, we think far more about what we're going to say next than actually listening to what's being said. Active listening is a technique that operates on a couple of different levels. First and foremost, it serves to clarify what's being said and understood. Second, it tends to slow things down a bit, allowing for a little breathing room in the argument.

Active listening basically works like this: You listen to what someone tells you, and then you repeat back what you understand them to be saying in your own words. The idea is to try to clear up anything that might have gotten lost in translation. Now, you don't necessarily do this with every sentence the person utters. That would just be annoying. But check in with them throughout the conversation, paraphrasing or summarizing what you understand them to have said and asking if you're correct. That last bit is important, too. Give them the opportunity to correct you if there's anything you misunderstood.

GIVE FEEDBACK

No one wants to talk to a brick wall. Show them you're listening by providing some appropriate feedback. A simple nod of the head can be enough to let the person know you're paying attention. There are times when you just want to keep the speaker talking, perhaps in the hopes that they'll reveal more information than they might have originally intended. In those cases, it is crucial for the speaker to receive some sort of feedback so they know they're not being ignored.

Even if you already know the answers, asking questions about minor details is an excellent way to keep the conversation going. Occasionally, doing so may even shed light on a heretofore unknown tidbit that could prove important later.

DON'T INTERRUPT

How many times do you tell your children to stop interrupting you? How many times did your own parents tell you the same thing? There are a couple of reasons why we often find ourselves cutting someone off in a conversation. First, we human beings are pretty much all self-centered jerks. We would much rather talk about ourselves than listen to another person talk about themselves.

Think about it. When someone relates a story to you, one of the most typical responses is to respond with a story about yourself that somehow relates to what they said. What happens, though, is you spend a lot of time thinking about your response and getting impatient because you want to share it. While this is happening, you're losing interest in what the speaker is telling you. Finally, you reach a point where you can't hold it in any longer and you interrupt because your story is so much better than theirs. At least, that's what you think.

The second reason is impatience. If you believe you can predict where the conversation is heading, you may try to speed things along. The problem is, your guess might be wrong and by interrupting, you spoil your chances of finding out what the other person truly wanted to share.

Sometimes, that impatience can come from your experience with the other person. You may have learned over time that they often complain about the same issues over and over, or they relate the same stories again and again. You may sometimes interrupt in an attempt to maintain your own sanity.

In any event, occasional interruptions are to be expected the average conversation. However, cutting the speaker off risks shutting them down completely. And for many people, that effect can linger for some time. If you want others to feel comfortable communicating with you, keep the interruptions to a minimum, no matter how justified you feel they may be.

BE BRIEF AND SPECIFIC

You know that person who, when asked to summarize a movie, details every single camera shot and recites every line of dialogue? Don't be that person. Keep your commentary short and to the point as much as possible. It's one thing if you're hanging out with a friend and shooting the breeze. It's quite another when you're trying to communicate with a relative stranger about a matter that could be rather important.

One of the quickest ways to lose someone's attention is to stray down rabbit holes that have little to nothing to do with the topic at hand.

TAILOR VOCABULARY TO THE AUDIENCE

Sometimes we forget our audience and use words and phrases that we should avoid, whether it's using harsh language in front of little ears or perhaps being extremely verbose and taking too much time to convey a point. Some people try to impress others with their vocabulary and will use a twenty-five-cent word when a five-cent one would do the job just as well.

That being said, there may be times when you'll find it necessary to attempt to intimidate your audience. Experience has shown me you can use your vocabulary skills then, to great effect. If you're dealing with someone who appears to be dimwitted, such as someone along the lines of the stereotypical schoolyard bully, using large words and complex sentence structure, provided you ensure they can still understand the gist of what you're saying, works rather well in many cases.

On the other hand, if you're speaking with someone who is rather articulate and at least appears reasonably intelligent, consider dialing your own dialogue down a few notches and speak to them in harsh tones, tossing in a few colorful words and phrases every now and again. Believe it or not, I've seen this do the trick when other approaches have failed. While I know many very intelligent people who can also curse like a sailor on shore leave, doing so amongst their peers often makes those people uncomfortable. If the goal is to ruffle the feathers of the other person, this approach might do it handily.

DON'T ASSUME UNDERSTANDING

A big mistake many people make is to assume their message was received clearly and understood completely. This is sort of the opposite of active listening. When you were the listener, you paraphrased what you heard and asked if you understood the other person correctly. As the speaker, you should also check in with the listener. Simply asking if they understood what you said can suffice in some cases. If it is a complicated issue, though, you may want to take a moment or two to ensure they've gotten the gist of what you said by asking them to repeat it to you.

BE CONFIDENT

If you want someone to listen to you, pay close attention to you, and believe you, then you need to be confident with what you communicate and how you say it. Keep your head up and speak loudly enough to be heard easily. Don't mumble and don't beat around the bush. Say what you have to say with complete conviction.

Avoid phrases like "In my opinion…" We know it is your opinion since you're the one expressing it. Instead, what you have to say should be said as though it is fact, with complete and utter confidence. There may come a time when you need another person to take what you have to say as iron-clad fact. That won't happen if you're namby-pamby about it.

USE APPROPRIATE HUMOR

Back when I worked in security, I learned early on that humor can be a massively effective stress release. I found that if I could get a person I'd detained to at least chuckle, a tense situation would often defuse itself to a large degree. However, this approach isn't for everyone. You can either pull it off or you can't. There's no way to fake it.

Self-deprecating humor is often best, though you can occasionally get away with poking fun of the other person. You're not coming up with a long stand-up routine, either. A one-liner here or there will usually suffice. All you're doing is releasing some of the pressure to keep things from exploding.

Chapter 9

BODY LANGUAGE

It is fairly common knowledge that the majority of our interpersonal communication occurs nonverbally. It isn't just *what* is said but *how* it is said that conveys the entire message. In fact, sometimes the message is left unspoken yet understood completely. A teenage boy tiptoeing into the house an hour past curfew to find his mother standing in the kitchen, her arms crossed and a foot tapping on the floor, knows beyond the shadow of a doubt how she feels about the situation.

The applications of body language interpretation in a survival setting are limited only by your imagination. For starters, anything that will assist group members to get along a little better is certainly welcome. A disaster and the subsequent recovery period are going to be filled with stress. By improving the communication skills of your group members, you will hopefully minimize disagreements and arguments.

On top of that, you or your group may find it necessary to network and interact with other groups in the area. By keeping your eyes and ears open, paying attention to the subtle cues in body language, you may find it easier to determine the truth in what you're being told.

Body language is an extremely vast and complicated subject, one that books, seminars, and college courses have covered. With that in mind, I'll scratch the surface of the topic here.

CONTEXT IS CRUCIAL

Perhaps the single most important rule that applies to interpreting body language is that no individual gesture, movement, or expression is definitive. That would be like picking one sentence out of the latest Stephen King doorstop and trying to use it to unravel the entire plot. Reading body language consists of picking up on various clues and seeing how they relate to one another, then adding them together to reach a conclusion.

One reason this is important is because everyone has their own little quirks and tics, which might mean something entirely different when exhibited by someone else. For example, wringing hands is often a sign of nervousness or guilt. However, some people are just naturally fidgety and have a difficult time sitting still. In fact, if you *really* weren't

RIGHT BRAIN VERSUS LEFT BRAIN

It is fairly well known that the left side of the brain is more analytical and the right side more creative. This can be used while studying body language. See, if you're talking to someone and ask them a question like, "What happened to you last week?" and they look up and to their left, odds are they are scanning their memory for the answer. However, if they look up and to their right, they are accessing the creative centers of the brain to come up with a cool, or at least believable, story.

As with anything else regarding body language, this is just one small tidbit to consider in the grand scheme of things.

paying attention, you may have missed the person squeezing out a small dollop of hand moisturizer, and rather than being nervous about the topic of conversation, they're simply working the lotion into their hands.

Environment is also a factor. Let's say you work in Human Resources and are in charge of interviewing people for new positions in the company. If you routinely keep your office as cold as an ice box, you might mistakenly think all of the job candidates are closed off or disagreeable because of their crossed arms and legs when, in fact, they are just cold. Sweating could indicate nervousness, but it could also indicate they made a bad decision by wearing a wool sweater instead of a light jacket. The inability to make eye contact could indicate dishonesty, but it could also be because of the 87 boldly colored framed pictures on the wall behind you.

ARE EYES WINDOWS TO THE SOUL?

Maybe, maybe not. But they can be indicators of deception. One of the first things to watch for when speaking with someone is their eyes. Most of us know that people tend to avoid making eye contact when they lie. However, persistent eye contact can also be an indicator, as the person doing the lying no doubt knows that looking away might be seen as dishonest. So, quite often, they will overcompensate and hold your gaze for long periods of time.

Eye contact is also sometimes used as a bullying or intimidation tool. If someone stares hard at you, are you likely to see them as friendly or antagonistic? Sure, it sort of depends on the situation and their facial expression. If they look angry, odds are you're in trouble. However, even if the person is outwardly friendly, uncommonly relentless eye contact can be just plain creepy.

Generally speaking, if the person is being truthful and is actively engaged in the conversation, their eyes will focus on your face 75 to 80 percent of the time. It won't always be eye-to-eye contact, of course. Their eyes will roam about your face but return to your eyes regularly.

BODY LANGUAGE IS OFTEN SYMBOLIC

The heart of body language is that our bodies try to convey the truth, even when our mouths don't. For example, if someone is lying, you might find one of their hands creeping up to cover their mouth. People also tend to cover their tender bits when nervous or tense. Crossing of the legs and hands covering the throat are also signs of deception.

Crossing the arms in front of the chest or stomach is another defensive movement. It indicates the desire to protect oneself from harm. The person in such a stance may either feel threatened by what you are saying or feel as though their lies are going to lead to bad things.

On the other hand, if they sit with their legs open and their hands in their lap, they are relaxed and likely speaking truthfully. Their posture shows that they feel safe in your presence and aren't afraid to expose themselves to you.

Keep an eye on feet, too. Pointing the feet toward the exit is a sign someone wants to get the conversation over with and leave. The same thing applies to shuffling feet.

PHYSIOLOGICAL INDICATORS

The human body reacts to stress in certain predictable ways. The polygraph, or lie detector, measures some of these physiological changes or reactions, and the results are interpreted by the operator to determine honesty. The validity of polygraph testing is in dispute, but that isn't because the testing doesn't work. Rather, it is because of the high possibility of false positive readings. In other words, the machine only measures the level of anxiety being experienced by the subject, not why they are feeling that way. They could be lying their fool's head off—or they could just really need to use the bathroom.

You might not have access to a polygraph, but you can certainly pay attention to the same body indicators of stress and deception. Think about it—what happens to you when you get anxious or nervous? For starters, your pulse rate goes up. In fact, for many people, the heart begins jackhammering to an almost ridiculous degree. Of course, you'd need a stethoscope to check the heart rate. Or would you?

So long ago it feels like a past life, I worked in security management. Part of my job involved interviewing employees suspected of dishonesty, specifically various types of theft. I recall one interview in particular where my boss and I were speaking to a cashier supervisor. My boss conducted the actual interview as I sat off to the side observing. The cashier was calm, cool, and collected until we approached the subject of some money that was missing from one of the cash registers from the day before. I noticed her shirt collar start bouncing up and down as her heart began to pound. There were many other indicators of guilt, too, not the least of which was the videotape we had of her taking the money. But I'll always remember the way that shirt collar was almost vibrating due to her heart rate.

Respiration, or breathing rate, also increases under stress. Of course, this is easier to spot than a change in heart rate. Keep what I've said all along in mind, though, and take exterior influences into account. If someone has just walked up a steep hill, they're going to be out of breath whether they're lying to you or not. Watch for sudden changes in their breathing, which means you need to pay attention to it from the outset so you'll notice the difference. The change is often subtle, too. It likely won't be that they are suddenly gasping for breath. Instead, their voice may change a bit as their breathing becomes a little shallower.

In addition to heart rate and breathing rate, a polygraph also measures galvanic skin resistance. Basically, this is a measurement of how well the skin conducts electricity. People who are under stress tend to sweat. This moisture on the surface of the skin allows electricity to flow more easily than if the skin were dry.

You're not likely to have a polygraph, but you can watch for an increase in perspiration. If the person in question looks like the spokesperson for a new antiperspirant but suddenly has sweat rolling off of them, either the heat just kicked on in the room or they aren't happy with the direction of the conversation.

Of course, many people can "beat" a polygraph. There are two ways, often used in conjunction, to go about doing so. The first is to remain as calm and friendly as possible, thus reducing or even eliminating any indications of stress or anxiety. The second is to attempt to give false positives to the control questions, thus making it seem as though the responses to the "real" questions read as honest. For example, when asked questions about their name, address, and other routine information, a subject might think about something scary or perhaps go so far as to prick themselves with a needle in order to increase heart rate, breathing rate, or perspiration. Later, when they need to lie to cover something up, the polygraph won't give a positive reading.

One more physiological indicator, though not one that would be measured by a polygraph, is a dry mouth. Often, nervousness leads to a decrease in saliva production. If the person to whom you are speaking seems to have trouble swallowing or is constantly licking their lips, this could be a sign of deception. If, however, it is the middle of August on a bright sunny day, they might just be thirsty. Remember to take the whole picture into account rather than focusing on one possible indicator of dishonesty.

TRUST YOUR GUT

"I knew there was something off about him." How many times have you had that thought? How many times have you had a bad feeling about a person, but couldn't pin down the reason, only to find out later that your suspicion was justified? This is intuition, something you grasp or know without conscious thought.

Quite often, the subconscious picks up on little clues and signals without our realizing it. The brain interprets these indicators and renders a decision seemingly out of nowhere. We experience this in many areas of our lives, from narrowly avoiding a traffic accident to making a snap judgment about the young person at the front door asking for your child. You won't be correct 100 percent of the time, of course. That young man might actually be a very nice, polite, and thoughtful person, but the lip piercing and bright green hair threw you off.

The point is, listen to your gut. Pay attention to your instincts. Your subconscious is trying to tell you something and odds are pretty good that whatever it is saying is important.

Chapter 10

CONFLICT RESOLUTION

Interpersonal conflict is not inherently bad. In fact, it can be quite good and helpful, as I'll discuss in a bit. While most people prefer to avoid conflict as much as possible, the reality is we have to deal with it on a regular basis.

So why include a chapter on conflict resolution in a prepper book? Well, here's the thing. Stress tends to lead to arguments in the best of times. Can you imagine the amount of stress likely to be present in our lives after a major disaster? By taking the time now to learn how to defuse arguments, you and your group will be much better off down the road. Plus, these are skills you can use just about every single day.

Before I get too much further, let me clarify the type of conflict I'm discussing here. When I say "interpersonal conflict," I'm talking about arguments or disagreements that happen between yourself and those around you. I'd also include those instances where you're a third party, or referee, to a discussion between two or more others in your family or group. In other words, I'm not talking about some sort of armed confrontation with a group of strangers intent on taking your supplies or anything else along those lines.

With that cleared up, let's look at a few different ways to defuse conflict.

STRATEGIES

Several different strategies exist for dealing with conflict, each with its pros and cons. As you practice these approaches, you'll get a feel for which ones to use for different situations as well as when you're dealing with certain individuals in your group or family.

Concession

Some conflicts just aren't worth the time or energy to continue. If surrendering the point does you no harm and will end the argument, this may be the best approach to take. After all, you have a life to lead and spending inordinate amounts of time arguing about the little things does nobody much good.

You might also consider the fact that, well, you just might be wrong. I'm sure that's happened at least once in your life, right? That moment in a heated debate when you realize you have been vehemently defending a point or side that's entirely wrong is one of the worst feelings in the world. Surrender is likely your best option at that point.

Remember, too, that surrendering in an interpersonal conflict doesn't reduce your value as a human being, make you less of a person, or cause baldness. It won't make others point and laugh at you. It can be difficult to do, no question about it. But, in many cases, it truly is an instance of taking the high road.

Consensus

If the conflict involves a group of people, taking a vote and letting the majority rule can be a viable option in some cases. The important thing here is to clarify things at the outset that the outcome of the vote is what everyone will follow, no matter what.

A great way to use this approach is to allow each side a bit of time to state their case and make their argument to the group as a whole. The vote can be public or private as the circumstances and issues warrant.

It is also helpful to have at least one person act as an independent judge of sorts. Someone without a stake in the fight who can help guide the process along. Ideally, this person will be someone the group as a whole respects, whether they are the de facto leader of the group or not.

THE TWO MOST IMPORTANT WORDS TO REMEMBER

A very smart guy told me a secret a while back. The two most important words in any interpersonal relationship are "I understand." With that deceptively simple phrase, you are telling the other person:

1. You have heard what they said.
2. You comprehend their meaning.
3. You are validating how they feel about the situation.

This doesn't necessarily mean you agree with them. In fact, you might feel the exact opposite of how they feel about the topic at hand. What you are doing, though, is making sure the other person knows you are not blowing them off or ignoring their perspective. With those two words, they will know you are paying attention and that you are actively engaged in the conversation. Of course, don't say them unless you mean it.

Mediation

This approach brings in a neutral third party to help determine a workable solution to the dilemma at hand. The mediator doesn't make the final decision. Instead, he or she assists the parties involved to better understand each point of view and come to an agreement.

The mediator's primary role is to keep the lines of communication open between the parties involved in the dispute as well as pass information back and forth when necessary. Again, the mediator doesn't get involved in the final solution; the parties involved do that themselves. This is a well-suited approach to parties who are open to resolution and willing to consider other points of view.

Arbitration

A cousin to mediation, arbitration also involves a third party. In this case, though, the third party is the final decision maker in the conflict. Think of the arbiter as a judge whose decision is, hopefully, final. He or she listens to the differing points of view and ideally makes a decision that is fair.

Generally speaking, the parties plead their case, so to speak, to an impartial judge or panel of judges. Arbitration is not unlike a court hearing in that respect. Each side works to prove they are right and the other wrong.

A key element of this approach is that the parties involved must agree to abide by the arbiter's decision. Arbitration works well in situations where the parties involved can't seem to communicate with one another without conversations immediately devolving into shouting matches or they otherwise cannot seem to get along.

Compromise

This is probably the most common approach to interpersonal conflicts. The basic premise is to meet in the middle. Each side gains something by giving something else up. While the parties may become resentful or angry about having to lessen their demands, it isn't always possible for one side or the other to get everything they want regardless.

The downside is that compromise is often overused in our daily lives. We have a tendency to turn to compromise first when in many cases it isn't the ideal approach. If it is used too often, it can lead to feelings of resentment and anger as the parties feel as though they never fully win an argument or dispute.

Compromise is an excellent option when it isn't feasible, or even remotely possible, for both sides to get their way entirely. Often, it is used to break a stalemate. If nothing else, discussing a potential compromise can open the channels of communication.

Collaboration

If all parties involved are willing to openly discuss the matter and their demands could conceivably be met, collaboration is the way to go. It is truly a win/win approach. In order to be successful, though, the parties have to be willing to work together to find a solution that benefits everyone. If there is negativity or ill will on the part of even one participant, collaboration won't work.

Collaboration is probably the most difficult approach to try because it is rare that all sides of the dispute will not only be open to working together on the solution but also be able to find a common ground that gives everyone what they want. However, in cases where those elements all come together, the results can be amazing.

Competition

This is essentially a win-at-all costs approach. Of the different techniques presented here, it is the least likely to succeed in most situations. Yet, it is also the first one many people attempt. Think of it as saying "my way or the highway." The winner in this argument gets everything they want, whatever the consequences.

The competition approach should only be used when you know in your heart and soul that you are right and that if you concede, there will be grave repercussions either now or later. Examples include times when you are being bullied into doing something you feel is wrong or when a decision must be made immediately for the safety or security of the family or group.

While this approach could get you what you want in the dispute, the repercussions could be serious. Quite often, the "loser" will be resentful, especially if this way of handling interpersonal conflicts is the routine rather than the exception. This can lead to more heated disputes down the road, even over issues that are fairly trivial in nature.

LEADERSHIP AND CONFLICT RESOLUTION

Keep in mind that resolving conflict is part and parcel of effective leadership. Whether you or someone else is in charge, that leader needs to take an active role in keeping things running smoothly on an interpersonal level. All too often, leaders think their job is the high-level stuff, the big decisions that are just too complicated for the common folk to understand.

In reality, an effective leader knows he or she must be able to rely upon the group as a whole. Interpersonal conflict, left unchecked, divides and fractures the group. If disputes aren't resolved quickly and appropriately, group members will lose faith and trust in the leader, *whether he or she is actually responsible for the conflict or not.*

Think back to the most recent election. It doesn't matter if it was presidential or local. How did you decide which candidate to choose? Sure, you considered the big issues, that's just smart. But, I'm willing to bet you also gave some thought to your overall quality of life under the current administration. If you weren't satisfied with it, your vote may have gone to someone else. Is your mayor really to blame for higher prices at the grocery store? Nope, not even a little. But a small part of your subconscious holds him or her responsible because it happened on their watch.

An effective leader will also be able to tell the difference between interpersonal conflict and manufactured drama. Many groups and certainly most families have at least one person who frequently seems self-serving and willing to do whatever it takes to be the center of attention. Conflict strictly for the sake of attention is nothing more than drama. Here's the thing, though. Like genuine disputes, this needs to be addressed as soon as possible. But the manner in which it is handled differs from "real" arguments. The drama king or queen needs to be taken aside and spoken with about their behavior. It needs to be made clear that unless there is a stage, costumes, and a director involved, drama cannot and will not be tolerated.

A good leader will also view conflict as an opportunity rather than a roadblock. Conflict, when handled effectively, can serve to clear the air between those involved. Quite often, the dispute on the surface is actually hiding a deep-seated issue. There might be a long-standing sense of favoritism for a specific group or family member, leading others to resent them. The leader needs to address that sort of thing as soon as it becomes known.

Conflict often brings about change, which can be a very good thing. Disputes can lead to new ways of doing things, whether they're performing tasks or just ensuring dissenting voices are heard. In other words, conflict can cause innovation. A true leader knows this and embraces conflict as a means to make the group better.

One last thing about conflict and leadership. Some disputes are best handled with a stern voice and a "cut-the-crap" attitude. However, if that's the standard method used in all situations, the group is going to lose faith in the leader rather quickly. Of course, a lot depends upon the types of people in the group. If, for example, every member is a combat veteran, they are likely to handle such a "command-and-control" leadership style rather well. However, a group consisting primarily of laypeople, office workers, and homemakers will probably chafe at such treatment. This in and of itself will lead to resentment, anger, and ever more conflict within the group. Food for thought.

We are all human beings. As such, we come to the table with our own opinions and perspectives, our own preconceived notions of how things ought to be. We have feelings and emotions. Interpersonal conflict happens all the time, no matter how close-knit the group or family. Knowing how to effectively handle conflict makes the group stronger and ensures it will stand the test of time, come what may.

FINAL THOUGHTS

While emergency communication might sound like a secondary requirement, falling as it does after water, food, and shelter on the list of basic needs, being able to send and receive information is indeed critical. It is important to have the ability to call for help when necessary, as well as coordinate rescue efforts.

On top of that, a psychological component is at work here. Even if all your life-sustaining needs are being met—you're fed, hydrated, and out of the elements—many people will find it comforting to be able to commiserate with another human being, not to mention giving and receiving advice about this, that, or the other thing. Like it or not, we're pack animals and wired to seek the company of others of like mind.

Obviously, communicating with others shouldn't be limited to emergencies. Networking with other preppers in your area will benefit you in many ways. I'm not saying to invite strangers over and give them tours of your preps. But think beyond the paranoia. Most emergencies you'll face won't mark the end of the world. They'll be temporary power outages, blizzards, and earthquakes, perhaps with some civil unrest sprinkled on top. As such, having people you can call for help when your generator isn't cooperating or if you're stranded at work and need someone who can check on your home or family will be extremely comforting.

Take the time to learn how to use your chosen methods of emergency communication so you'll have the capacity to use those tools under a variety of conditions as well as under stress.

Remember, too, that communication skills are just as important as hardware and software. All of the tools, gadgets, and gizmos in the world won't do you much good if you're not able to express yourself effectively and pass along information efficiently. Practice makes perfect.

Above all, keep in mind that communication, by its very nature, involves other human beings. Take each new bit of information you learn after a crisis hits with a grain of salt until it is verified. People have a tendency to exaggerate or embellish. Some sources are more reliable than others, and it is only through making contacts with those around you as well as listening to a variety of sources that you'll learn the facts.

RESOURCES

Organizations

ARRL

www.arrl.org

The Amateur Radio Relay League is the largest amateur radio organization in the United States. It has well over 150,000 members. Their website is packed with excellent information on everything from ham license test preparation to product reviews. There is even an extensive message board where you can communicate with fellow radio enthusiasts from all over the world. The ARRL also acts as the voice of amateur radio operators in front of regulatory bodies when the need arises.

Local clubs

There are too many county or municipal level radio clubs to list here. Clubs that are affiliated with the ARRL may be found by searching this link: www.arrl.org/find-a-club. Otherwise, simply do a Google search with your county name and "radio club" or a similar term.

Suppliers

American Science & Surplus

www.sciplus.com

American Science & Surplus is, well, you sort of have to see it to understand. As a surplus outlet, the products they offer change frequently. The store is a hobbyist's dream, though. You name the obscure electronics part and I'm betting they have it, probably in three colors. They offer a lot more than just electronics, too. Everything from office supplies and toys to chemistry equipment and military gear, they have it all. If you come across one of their brick and mortar stores in your travels, don't miss the opportunity browse the shelves in person.

Baofeng

www.baofengradio.us

For quite some time now, the Baofeng UV-5R has been an ideal option for the ham operator looking for something small yet powerful. It is fairly inexpensive and is a great radio for someone just getting started.

Cobra

www.cobra.com

Cobra established itself as a leader in portable CB radios quite some time ago. Their handheld radios have stood the test of time. Their two-way radio sets are also worth considering.

Eton

www.etoncorp.com/en

Eton is well known for their emergency communications products, particularly their emergency radios. They manufacturer other disaster-related products as well, including a water-activated emergency light.

Goal Zero

www.goalzero.com

Goal Zero has become the go-to source for portable solar power. They offer a wide range of options, all of them guaranteed to keep your small electronics powered up and ready to go.

Kaito Electronics, Inc.

www.kaitousa.com

Kaito has long been a favorite brand for emergency radios. Their Voyager radio is particularly popular amongst the prepper crowd, owing to its six different power options (crank, USB, battery, rechargeable battery pack, solar, AC).

SunJack

www.sunjack.com

SunJack offers a few different excellent options for solar power. I'm particularly a fan of their 14-watt portable solar panel system. Their Waterproof LightStick Powerbank is also pretty nifty.

Books

Emergency Power for Radio Communications, 2nd Edition, by Michael Bryce (ARRL, 2012)
A great introduction to alternative power systems, this book explains different available options, particularly for those looking at long-term, grid-down scenarios.

Ham Radio for Dummies, 2nd Edition, by H. Ward Silver (John Wiley & Sons, 2013)
I'm a big fan of the For Dummies series. In this book, H. Ward Silver covers everything from getting your ham license to setting up your first radio shack to how to use your gear to help during a crisis or disaster.

The ARRL Ham Radio License Manual, by ARRL, Inc. (ARRL, 2014)
This book covers everything you need to know to get started in amateur radio, including studying for and passing the Technician Class license exam. The license exam pulls 35 questions from a large pool. This book contains all of the possible questions you'll see on the exam, along with the correct answers. Study the book and learn the correct answers for all of those questions and you'll be golden when you take the exam.

INDEX

ACKNOWLEDGMENTS

As always, a huge thanks to my ever-supportive wife, Tammy. Without your help, guidance, and putting up with my antics, I wouldn't be where I am today. I love you, Sweets.

To my boys, excuse me, my young men, thank you for making me laugh and showing me there's hope for the future.

Special thanks to Dan Paullin for his input on CB radio communication.

To Chris Golden, I'll always have your back, Brother.

To John McCann, a colleague and friend, thank you for your support, your input, and most of all, for always speaking your mind rather than saying what you think people want to hear.

Last, but certainly not least, thank you to all of my readers who have picked up one or more of my books in the last few years. If it weren't for you, I'd have to go out and get a real job.

ABOUT THE AUTHOR

Jim Cobb is the author of several books focused on disaster readiness, such as *Prepper's Long-Term Survival Guide*, *Countdown to Preparedness*, *Prepper's Financial Guide*, and the #1 Amazon bestselling *Prepper's Home Defense*. He has been a student of survivalism and prepping for about thirty years. He is the owner of SurvivalWeekly.com, a rather popular disaster readiness resource.

Jim and his family reside in the upper Midwest and he is currently working on several more books.

Made in the USA
Las Vegas, NV
10 October 2024